CAMPAIGN • 200

JAPAN 1945

From Operation *Downfall* to Hiroshima and Nagasaki

CLAYTON K S CHUN   ILLUSTRATED BY JOHN WHITE

Series editors Marcus Cowper and Nikolai Bogdanovic

First published in 2008 by Osprey Publishing
Midland House, West Way, Botley, Oxford OX2 0PH, UK
443 Park Avenue South, New York, NY 10016, USA
E-mail: info@ospreypublishing.com

A CIP catalog record for this book is available from the British Library.

ISBN 978 184603 284 4

Editorial by Ilios Publishing, Oxford, UK (www.iliospublishing.com)
Page layout by The Black Spot
Typeset in Sabon and Myriad Pro
Index by Alison Worthington
Originated by PPS Grasmere Ltd., Leeds
Cartography by The Map Studio
Bird's-eye view artworks by The Black Spot
Printed in China through Worldprint Ltd.

08 09 10 11 12   10 9 8 7 6 5 4 3 2 1

FOR A CATALOG OF ALL BOOKS PUBLISHED BY OSPREY MILITARY
AND AVIATION PLEASE CONTACT:

NORTH AMERICA
Osprey Direct, c/o Random House Distribution Center, 400 Hahn Road,
Westminster, MD 21157
E-mail: info@ospreydirect.com

ALL OTHER REGIONS
Osprey Direct UK, P.O. Box 140 Wellingborough, Northants, NN8 2FA, UK
E-mail: info@ospreydirect.co.uk

www.ospreypublishing.com

ARTIST'S NOTE

Readers may care to note that the original paintings from which the color
plates in this book were prepared are available for private sale. The
Publishers retain all reproduction copyright whatsoever. All enquiries
should be addressed to:

John White, 5107 C Monroe Road, Charlotte, NC 28205, USA

The Publishers regret that they can enter into no correspondence upon
this matter.

LINEAR MEASUREMENTS

Distances, ranges and dimensions are mostly given in the contemporary
US system of inches, feet, yards and statute miles rather than metric:

feet to meters:	multiply feet by 0.3048
yards to meters:	multiply yards by 0.9144
miles to kilometers:	multiply miles by 1.6093

ACKNOWLEDGMENTS

I could not have completed this book without the outstanding support
of several individuals and organizations. The following people willingly
gave much help and advice throughout the process. My editors Nikolai
Bogdanovic and Marcus Cooper from Ilios Publishing continued to provide
superb coordination and oversight of the project. Additionally, John
White's excellent artistic abilities brought life to the story of Japan 1945.
The Army Heritage and Education Center at the U.S. Army War College,
Carlisle Barracks, PA and the Albert F. Simpson Historical Research Center,
Maxwell AFB, AL gave me invaluable help answering many questions.
Finally, I want to thank my family for their patience during this project.

THE WOODLAND TRUST

Osprey Publishing are supporting the Woodland Trust, the UK's leading
woodland conservation charity, by funding the dedication of trees.

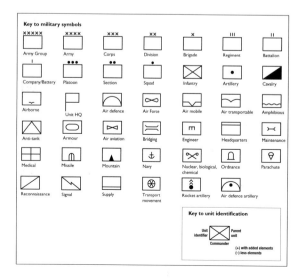

CONTENTS

The Pacific Theater, February 1945

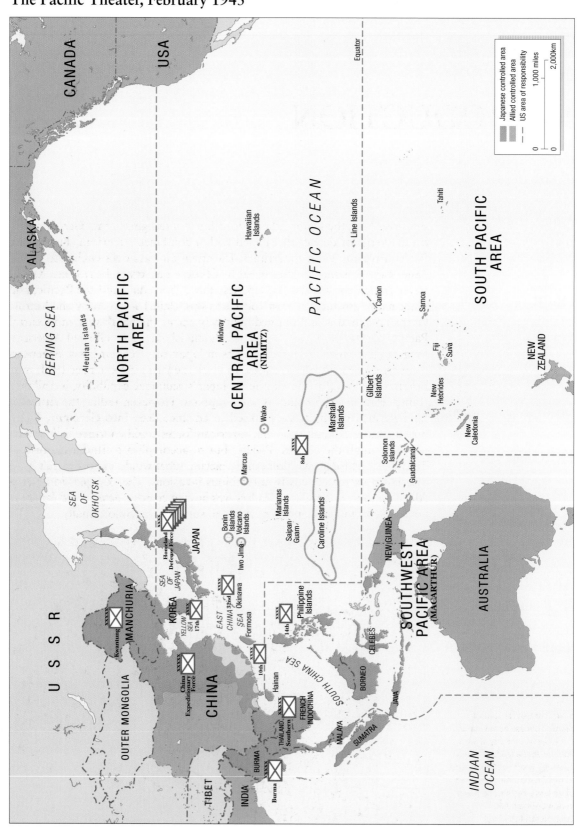

INTRODUCTION

By early 1945, the senior Allied leadership had recognized that Germany was on the verge of defeat, threatened with a combined American, British and Soviet drive into German territory. The attention was now switched to Japan. American, British, Commonwealth, Chinese and other forces had fought bitter campaigns against the Japanese throughout Asia and the Pacific, and made major advances against Tokyo's troops. United States Army and Marine Corps units had island-hopped their way across the Southwest and Central Pacific, getting close to the Japanese home islands. This allowed American long-range bombers to attack targets in Japan on a regular basis. American submarines, which had first started to blockade Japan in December 1941, now began to tighten their death grip on Japan's economic capability, its military transportation system and its food supplies. However, unlike the situation facing Allied ground forces poised to advance deep into Germany, Japan posed a more difficult problem. American forces could continue their march north through the Central Pacific, but to accomplish a similar capture of Tokyo, Allied forces would need to execute what would almost certainly be a series of extremely costly amphibious invasions. The key question facing Allied national and military leaders was how to coerce a determined Japanese government, military and population to surrender unconditionally.

In any contest for control of the Japanese home islands, the Allies' superiority in arms and *matériel* would be telling. Japanese heavy weapons, such as this IJA machine gun, were often less effective and fewer in number than Allied equivalents. (US Army)

ABOVE, LEFT
US Army Air Forces (USAAF) officers hoped to use strategic bombing as a powerful tool in the Pacific Theater. The B-29 would find fame as a weapons delivery platform that would help end the war. (US Air Force)

ABOVE, RIGHT
America fought a brutal hand-to-hand campaign to liberate the Pacific, as demonstrated by this scene from Leyte's recapture in 1944. (DOD)

The United States had been at war for more than three years by January 1945. The nation had sacrificed its military, population and economy fighting an extensive two-front war. Although heavy attrition had worn down Japanese military capability by 1945, a fresh round of Pacific amphibious invasions from the Philippines and Central Pacific had demonstrated that imperial Japanese military units would not surrender easily. Allied leaders could see a rush to end the war would be costly. Britain and her Commonwealth allies had fought alongside America throughout the Pacific; these countries had endured war since September 1939, and their resources were depleted. China was still under occupation while Nationalist and Communist forces struggled among themselves and against the common foe of the Japanese. How to end the war became a difficult challenge. Political and military conferences among the Allies seemed to follow a singular approach: a methodical defeat of Japanese forces on the home islands of Kyushu and Honshu, followed by the occupation of Tokyo. Still, Japanese forces maintained many, albeit weakened, units throughout Asia and the Pacific. Taking Tokyo might not guarantee the nation's defeat, as experience had taught the Allies that many Japanese soldiers, sailors and airmen would fight to the death. The Allies had to find a way to ensure they would surrender.

Japanese political and military leaders seemed, in public, unified in their desire to fight to the death. However, mounting losses and the destruction of Japanese cities by bombing were hard to hide and might mean the very destruction of Japan as a nation. There was a small but growing movement of Foreign Ministry officials and others who believed surrender was preferable to the type of end facing Germany, one that involved the destruction and occupation of the nation. These officials believed that a negotiated surrender would leave some territory under Japanese sovereignty. To these "peace" advocates capitulation was a goal, but not with the unconditional terms that the Americans, British and Chinese had sought. The most important aspect in their mind was keeping intact Japan's symbolic essence: the emperor and the imperial system. Opposing viewpoints recalled that Japanese military forces had executed spectacular victories in 1941 and 1942. Although Tokyo had suffered horrendous losses since Midway, its ground and naval units had not been totally broken. Japan's survival was still possible.

President Harry S. Truman's decision to use the new weapon of the atomic bomb twice against Japan continues to affect US national security policy and her international relations to this day, and the process itself provides a valuable insight into the way decisions were made under wartime pressures. Many US War Department officials viewed the atomic bomb as little more than a larger explosive device, with no wider significance; conventional strategic bombing had already leveled Dresden, Tokyo and other Axis cities, so what was so special about the atomic bomb? Many officials were also looking to the future and the postwar era, and sought means to demonstrate the relevance of their particular branches of service. An amphibious invasion would demonstrate the need for the US Army and Marine Corps, to protect the nation and win wars. Blockading Japan and bombarding her with surface-ship firepower and carrier aircraft would prove that naval forces could bring decisive results. Likewise, the air forces could claim that the use of bombers had broken the will and ability of the Japanese to continue the struggle. However, American forces that took the Philippines, Iwo Jima and Okinawa were shocked at the ferocity of the fanatical Japanese defense. The American and British political and military leadership had felt an invasion was the faster and most likely way to force a Japanese surrender. Although other American military leaders advocated alternative ways to defeat Japan, such as the opening of a second front by the Soviets (unlike Germany, the Japanese were fighting on only one major front against the Americans, and so opening another might make Japan's defeat quicker and less costly) an invasion seemed imminent. However, numerous voices in the Allied command

American casualties at Iwo Jima and Okinawa shocked US President Truman. These losses had a profound effect on his decision whether to launch an invasion of the Japanese home islands. (DOD)

In the campaigns across the Pacific in 1944 and 1945, US soldiers and Marines had to evict Japanese defenders from strong defensive positions, such as this cave, which resulted in high casualties. One option for clearing such positions was to use flamethrowers and chemical weapons. (DOD)

questioned this plan, fearing Allied casualties in the tens of thousands. It was with these considerations in mind that the American president made one of the most difficult decisions of the entire war.

The atomic bomb was but one of a long list of many innovative weapons to emerge during World War II. Developed from experimentation with nuclear power, it was considered, at one point, to be merely an expensive experiment, and one that some American government officials thought wasteful. The US War Department gathered the greatest scientific and technical experts available and spent an unheard of $2 billion to design, develop and test a theory. The effort was based on the ideas and concepts developed by a handful of highly influential scientists, who believed that Germany was developing nuclear power, which could give Adolf Hitler a weapon of great magnitude. European scientific immigrants, such as Albert Einstein, Niels Bohr and Enrico Fermi, had sufficient credibility to persuade President Franklin D. Roosevelt to establish a program to build an atomic bomb. Intended for use against Germany, this scientific device ultimately became an instrument that helped end the war against Japan.

The views and opinions of the political, organizational, strategic and military leaders all contributed to the eventual, difficult decision to drop the atomic bomb – one that has been subject to debate ever since. The debate at the time focused on the best way to demonstrate the Allies' determination to get Japan to surrender quickly. At stake was the conduct of the largest amphibious invasion planned for World War II, which might cost thousands of Allied, and particularly American, lives, not to mention those of the Japanese defenders and civilians who might be killed or wounded. The enemy, fighting for its existence, could continue resistance for years, putting at risk prisoners of war, civilians living in occupied territories and the Allied populations throughout Asia and the Pacific. Once the initial decision was made to land military forces in Japan and occupy sacred territory, it would be risky to switch the focus from invasion to reliance on an as yet unproven weapon.

Although the atomic bomb was instrumental in demonstrating a new threat to the Japanese national existence, the use of nuclear weapons was not the only factor that forced Japan's surrender. Mounting Japanese losses caused by increased and more intensive attacks on the home islands, the nation's dwindling economic capability, the threat of invasion and the fact that Japan had now become the sole focus of Allied military power following Germany's capitulation all influenced the nation's leaders in Tokyo. Japan's empire was shrinking at an increasing rate, and she could not hold back the relentless advance of Allied military power. Allied senior political and military leadership agreed that the Japanese empire's rule was coming to an end, but came to the conclusion that a major shock to the Japanese might push them to surrender. The time for that shock would come on 6 August 1945.

CHRONOLOGY

1939

2 August   Albert Einstein contacts Roosevelt about the feasibility of constructing a nuclear weapon.

1942

18 April   United States first attacks Japanese territory with several strikes on Tokyo and other areas with the Doolittle Raid.

17 June   Roosevelt approves a program for research and development of nuclear weapons, later to become the Manhattan Project.

1944

15 June   First B-29 bombing of Japan on Yawata in Kyushu from China.

24 November   Bombing missions on Japan commence from the Marianas.

17 December   509th Composite Group (CG) formed.

1945

20 January   Emperor Hirohito sanctions plans to start homeland defense operations in Japan.

5 March   The American Joint War Plans Committee produces a preliminary plan for Operation *Downfall*.

9/10 March   Incendiary bombing mission destroys major portions of Tokyo.

1 April   American forces land on Okinawa. Operations declared ended in the Ryukyu Islands as of 2 July.

8 April   Japanese military commanders develop detailed plans for future *Ketsu-Go* operations.

12 April   Following the death of Franklin D. Roosevelt, Harry S. Truman becomes President of the United States. Truman first learns about the existence of the atomic bomb.

24 April   US Joint Chiefs of Staff recommend invasion option as the only viable alternative to ensure unconditional surrender.

26 April   509th CG personnel begin transfer to Tinian.

27 April   Targeting Committee formed to examine Japanese cities that could be bombed with nuclear weapons.

25 May   Joint Chiefs of Staff decide on Operation *Olympic*'s start date of 1 November 1945. Operation *Coronet* is to begin on 1 March 1946.

18 June   President Truman gives initial authorization for Operation *Downfall*, but retains the right of final approval prior to an invasion.

30 June	509th CG starts training missions from Tinian.
16 July	Successful plutonium bomb test at Trinity, New Mexico.
17 July	Potsdam Conference starts.
25 July	Truman authorizes dropping the atomic bomb on Japan.
26 July	Potsdam Declaration reiterates unconditional surrender terms.
30 July	USS *Indianapolis*, the ship that delivered the uranium fissonable material for the first nuclear weapon, Little Boy, to Tinian, is sunk.
31 July	Scientists, engineers and technicians assemble Little Boy on Tinian. The bomb is ready to use on 1 August.
2 August	Truman gives final approval to use Little Boy.

6 August (all times based on Tinian time)

0151hrs	Weather aircraft leave Tinian to reconnoiter targets.
0245hrs	*Enola Gay* takes off with Little Boy.
0555hrs	Tibbets reaches Iwo Jima and meets up with escort aircraft.
0815hrs	Hiroshima selected as the primary target.
0912hrs	*Enola Gay* begins bomb run at the initial point.
0915hrs	Little Boy is released. 43 seconds later, the bomb explodes over Hiroshima.
7 August	American and British radio broadcasts announce the use of an atomic bomb on Hiroshima and reiterate the demand for Tokyo to accept the Potsdam Declaration. A divided Japanese cabinet starts discussion on surrender.

9 August (all times based on Tinian time)

0349hrs	Sweeney starts mission with *Bockscar* to drop the second nuclear device, Fat Man, on the primary target of Kokura.
0900hrs	Sweeney approaches Yakusima.
1044hrs	*Bockscar* starts bomb run over Kokura, but cloud cover prevents a visual bombing run.
1150hrs	Sweeney arrives over Nagasaki.
1158hrs	Fat Man is released. 50 seconds later, the bomb detonates over Nagasaki. Soviet Union declares war on Japan. Soviet forces start operations against Japanese forces in Northeast Asia.
10 August	Emperor Hirohito initially agrees to accept the Potsdam Declaration with conditions.
12 August	Washington refuses to accept Tokyo's conditions to the Potsdam Declaration.
14 August	Largest conventional B-29 raid on Japan takes place. Japanese government accepts the Potsdam Declaration without conditions. Japanese military officers attempt *coup d'état* that fails.
2 September	Japan formally surrenders on board the USS *Missouri*.

OPPOSING COMMANDERS

US COMMANDERS

As Supreme Commander, Allied Expeditionary Force, General **Dwight D. Eisenhower** controlled Allied Western European operations. He could plan and execute strategy in a more effective and efficient manner than coordinating his efforts with several co-equal Allied commanders. In the Pacific, military commanders had control of geographic or functional areas of operation, which were all but independent of each other, and coordination between them was frequently limited. Only major decisions on Pacific strategy were, like the European theater, conducted at joint and multinational levels, but Eisenhower had a much greater influence on the final strategies used by American and British forces. In the Pacific, strategy was debated largely in Washington and involved many diverse players.

Following President Franklin D. Roosevelt's death on 12 April 1945, **Harry S. Truman** became president and commander-in-chief. American and

Under Franklin Roosevelt, Pacific strategy was principally developed by MacArthur and Nimitz. Here, MacArthur, Roosevelt, Leahy and Nimitz (left to right) discuss strategy in Hawaii in 1944. (DOD)

George C. Marshall oversaw strategy development for American Army forces in the Pacific. He was a strong supporter of an invasion of the Japanese home islands. (US Army)

British strategists had delayed developing a detailed Pacific strategy until Germany's demise seemed certain. Truman was at the center of much of the controversy in deciding which of the options America would use to force Tokyo's surrender: invasion, naval blockade and aerial bombardment, negotiated surrender, getting the Soviets to declare war, or the experimental atomic bomb. Truman had grown up in Missouri. He served in France during World War I as a National Guard field artillery captain. The future president was elected to the US Senate in 1934 and served as chairman of the Senate Special Committee to Investigate the National Defense Program. Ironically, this committee examined alleged waste and corruption cases by defense contractors. One of the cases Truman's committee considered involved a land deal near Hanford, Washington for a defense project, which involved developing nuclear materials for the atomic bomb as part of the Manhattan Project. Truman's committee was never given significant details about the highly classified project, and only after becoming president did he learn about the program. Truman would oversee the decisions to end the war in Europe, the seeking of an agreement between Britain, China and Russia about Japan, and the formation of a strategy to bring about Japan's surrender – which was one of the most difficult decisions of his presidency. In the postwar period, Truman went on to formulate America's early Cold War policies, and led the nation during the Korean War (1950–53).

One of the most influential members of Truman's cabinet was Secretary of War **Henry L. Stimson**. Stimson had, like Truman, served in World War I as an army officer and was a former secretary of state during the Taft administration. He had witnessed Japan's rise during the interwar period, especially its aggressive moves in China and its increasing challenge to American influence in the Pacific. He was also deeply involved in the discussion about invasion plans, the development of the atomic bomb and moves to encourage Japan's surrender. Stimson was concerned about excessive civilian casualties caused by the incendiary bombing attacks on Japan, and advocated encouraging the Japanese to accept Allied peace terms with modified unconditional surrender terms.

Chief of Staff of the Army General **George C. Marshall, Jr.** started a long and distinguished military career in 1902 with an assignment to the Philippines. He had seen service in the 1st Infantry Division during World War I and was later on General John J. Pershing's staff. Marshall had a number of interwar period assignments that would influence his selection of particular officers to key command and staff positions during World War II. Selected as Army chief of staff on 1 September 1939, Marshall oversaw the army's mobilization and expansion from 269,000 members in 1940 to 8,266,000 in 1945. He served as one of Roosevelt's key military advisers and was an instrumental member on the US Joint Chiefs of Staff and the Anglo-American Combined Chiefs of Staff. Marshall was an integral member of Truman's advisory team deciding on how to end the war with Japan, and strongly advocated an invasion. Marshall would later become Truman's secretary of state and following the outbreak of the Korean War he became Secretary of Defense. One of his crowning achievements was the Marshall Plan, which helped European recovery efforts after World War II. A true soldier-statesman, he would later be awarded the Nobel Peace Prize.

Fleet Admiral **Ernest J. King** held two unique positions simultaneously throughout World War II: Commander-in-Chief, US Fleet and Chief of Naval Operations. King was noted for his acerbic nature, but would create a wartime naval force second to none. When asked why he was selected to head the US Navy, he proclaimed: "When the going gets tough, they bring in the sons of bitches." After graduation from the Naval Academy in 1901, he served in several commands, seeing service in Cuba, Asia, as a Naval Academy instructor, during World War I and various other appointments. King's experience of submarines and naval aviation gave him a broad knowledge of naval operations. He believed that a combined blockade and bombardment against a weakened Japan in 1945 would bring it to capitulation, and argued against a direct invasion; instead, he advocated invading China, Formosa, Korea and other locations as an alternative to landings in Japan. These locations would allow American forces to establish bases for naval and air units to pummel Japanese targets and intensify any blockade. This option might have created just as many casualties as a Japanese landing, not to mention logistical problems, and could have mired the American nation in a large-scale land conflict on the Asian mainland. King focused closely on American naval power, and did not trust British wartime intentions.

Fleet Admiral **William D. Leahy** held a unique position, and had unparalleled access to first Roosevelt and then Truman as their chief of staff and personal adviser to the commander-in-chief. Leahy also acted as a quasi-chairman of the Joint Chiefs of Staff, a position in which he could arbitrate over major army, navy, or alliance issues between Marshall and King. The admiral was a former Chief of Naval Operations from 1937 to 1939 and had served as ambassador to Vichy France from January 1941 to March 1942 when he was recalled to active duty. Leahy opposed an invasion of Japan and also believed that developing the atomic bomb was a waste of time and resources, believing that nuclear weapons would never work.

General of the Army **Henry "Hap" Arnold** was Chief of the USAAF. Arnold started his career as an infantry officer after graduating from the US Military Academy in 1903. Arnold successfully completed flight training under the Wright brothers in 1911 and was the first official US Army aviator. Selected to head the Army Air Corps in 1938, he would later lead the expanded USAAF on 30 June 1941. Arnold had taken a special interest in the use of strategic bombardment in Europe and later against Japan. Victory through the use of airpower was a strategy Arnold championed through his use of long-range bombers to hammer Germany into submission, independent of land and naval actions. B-29 bomber operations against the Japanese became a further example of airpower's value. Arnold pushed for an expanded USAAF bombardment in lieu of an invasion. He knew that if airpower beat Japan, then the movement to create an independent postwar air force would be strengthened.

The Central and Southwest Pacific areas saw much of the focus of military action against the Japanese by American forces. China, Burma and India received limited attention, but those areas paled in comparison with the actions on Pacific islands and ocean areas. Two main military leaders commanded maritime, land and air units, based on geographic divisions. General **Douglas MacArthur** had extensive experience in the Pacific. After graduation from the US Military Academy in 1903, he was posted to the Philippines. MacArthur would later earn 31 decorations in World War I,

TOP
Henry "Hap" Arnold advocated the use of B-29 raids as an alternative to an invasion of Japan. The ultimate use of strategic bombardment came with the events at Hiroshima and Nagasaki. (US Air Force)

BOTTOM
Douglas MacArthur, Supreme Commander of the Allied Powers, was slated to lead any invasion of the Japanese home islands. He ultimately rebuilt Japan during the postwar American occupation. (DOD)

Leslie Groves led the Manhattan Project. He was heavily involved in the development, targeting and operational use of the two nuclear devices, Little Boy and Fat Man. (National Archives)

including the French Croix de Guerre, the Distinguished Service Cross and several Silver Stars that illustrated his individual bravery and valor in action. During the interwar period, MacArthur became the US Military Academy's superintendent and later the Army Chief of Staff. MacArthur moved to the Philippines as commander of US Army forces and took the position of adviser to the Philippine military after his retirement. Recalled to active duty after Pearl Harbor, he watched Japan conquer the Philippines. He was awarded the Congressional Medal of Honor for his efforts in the Philippines, but Roosevelt ordered him to Australia. Never forgetting this debacle, MacArthur strongly advocated actions to retake the Philippines and later an invasion of Japan. MacArthur was appointed Commander-in-Chief of the Southwest Pacific Area, which allowed him to control activities in that theater of operations. Truman appointed him as commander of all American Pacific Army forces in anticipation of a ground invasion of Japan. MacArthur's staff developed the detailed invasion plans. He would later become Supreme Commander for the Allied Powers in the Pacific; in this role, he accepted the Japanese surrender and led the occupation of the home islands. In the immediate postwar period, MacArthur rebuilt the political, military and economic structure of Japan. He would later lead United Nation forces during the Korean War, during which he was relieved of command by Truman for insubordination.

Competing with MacArthur for limited resources in the Pacific was Fleet Admiral **Chester W. Nimitz**. Having graduated from the US Naval Academy, Nimitz's distinguished naval career included service in both submarines and battleships. Nimitz replaced Admiral Husband E. Kimmel as the Pacific Fleet commander, and directed the many amphibious assaults in the Central Pacific. The capture of the Mariana Islands allowed direct B-29 attacks on Japanese cities. Under Nimitz, naval forces defeated Japanese forces up through Iwo Jima and Okinawa. These victories allowed American naval and air forces to expand attacks directly on the Japanese home islands, but the task was expensive in terms of men and material. Direct operations against Japan fell in Nimitz's theater of operations. In anticipation of an invasion of Japan, Nimitz was appointed as commander for American Pacific naval forces. MacArthur would control land activities in the Pacific, with cooperation from Nimitz's Marine Corps units, for a Japanese invasion. Nimitz was aware of efforts in February 1945 and of a special B-29 unit that would operate from the Marianas. This unit was readying itself to drop atomic bombs possibly on Japan. After the war, Nimitz was appointed Chief of Naval Operations in September 1945.

Although not a combat commander, Major General **Leslie R. Groves** oversaw all activities that allowed the United States to develop the atomic bomb. He graduated from the US Military Academy in 1918 but did not see combat in World War I. His military construction experience as an engineer provided him with excellent project management skills. Reporting directly to Secretary of War Stimson, he led a collection of civilian and military nuclear scientists, engineers, technical and administrative personnel to develop the atomic bomb – the Manhattan Project. He was also instrumental in guiding the project through Washington circles, and involved himself in the selection of targets for the atomic bomb. Prior to this assignment, Groves was one of the chief architects involved in the construction of the largest office building in the world, the Pentagon.

Colonel **Paul W. Tibbets, Jr.** had enlisted in the Army Air Corps in 1937. Tibbets had flown in the first B-17 raid from England to Rouen, France, had combat experience in North Africa, and was involved in the flight testing of the B-29 before his selection by Arnold in August 1944 to lead the 509th Composite Group (CG). This highly secretive unit was formed with a single mission: to deliver a nuclear weapon. Colonel Tibbets prepared the B-29s and crews in the United States and transferred the unit to its Pacific bases in Tinian, an island in the Marianas. Tibbets would later pilot a B-29 and drop the first atomic bomb. He would retire from the Air Force as a brigadier general.

JAPANESE COMMANDERS

Hirohito Michinomiya was born on 19 April 1901 and became the long-serving emperor of Japan on 25 December 1926, a position he retained throughout World War II. His role in Japan's surrender was key to silencing many militarists who wanted to defend Japan to the last person. Hirohito would make the unprecedented move to speak directly to the Japanese people to accept unconditional surrender. He would also reject claims of the divine status of emperors. Hirohito died in 1989.

Emperor Hirohito was the head of the Japanese government and was considered a living god by many of his subjects. (US Army)

 Admiral Baron Suzuki Kantaro was prime minister at the time of Japan's surrender. A Japanese Naval Academy graduate of 1887, he served in the First Sino-Japanese War and the Russo-Japanese War. After commanding destroyers, battlecruisers and battleships, Suzuki was made Vice Minister of the Navy in World War I. He was the target of an assassination attempt for his part in gaining acceptance of the London Naval Disarmament Treaty, which reduced Japan's naval strength relative to the United States and Great Britain. He would be responsible for gathering unanimous acceptance of the American unconditional surrender terms at the end of the war. He died in 1948.

 Togo Shigenori held the position of foreign minister at the start and the end of World War II; he resigned from the Foreign Ministry on 1 September 1942 over a disagreement with General Tojo Hideki about the creation of the Greater East Asia Ministry and Tojo's aggressive moves throughout Asia and the Pacific. Togo's doubts about Japan's chances of success in World War II never left him. He believed fervently that Japan should surrender. Togo was convicted as a war criminal and died in prison in 1950.

 By 1945 Japanese military planning and operations had become driven by desperation. Earlier in the war, **General Prince Higashikuni Naruhiko** had directed the General Defense Command, which was responsible for Imperial Japanese Army (IJA) homeland operations. The Imperial Japanese Army Air Force (IJAAF) lacked fuel, a supporting aircraft industry, trained pilots and undamaged airfields in 1945. The Japanese did have a large number of suicide attack aircraft. When the General Defense Command was disbanded, control of the defensive IJA forces fell to geographic commands. Higashikuni later took command of the IJA after Japan surrendered.

 Field Marshal Hata Shunroku became commander of the Second General Army. Hata led defensive forces in Kyushu, Shikoku and western portions of Honshu. Commissioned in 1901 as an artillery officer, he fought in the Russo-Japanese War, was an attaché to Germany in 1912, and observed military operations during World War I. He saw extensive service in China, was an aide to the emperor and later Army minister from 1939 to 1940. Hata then commanded the Chinese Expeditionary Army from 1941 to 1944. His assignment as Commander, Second General Army made him responsible for the

General Prince Higashikuni Naruhiko (left) served as the IJA's principal homeland defense commander. Despite efforts to build effective defenses, Allied bombers pummeled Japanese industry, military bases and cities late in the war. Higashikuni commanded the IJA following Japan's surrender. (US Army)

defense of Kyushu, the expected initial landing site of the American amphibious invasion of Japan. His command was stationed in Hiroshima in August 1945. The International Military Tribunal for the Far East convicted Hata as a war criminal, owing partly to atrocities committed by his troops in China, and sentenced him in 1948 to life imprisonment. He was paroled in 1955.

Supporting the defense of Japan was the First General Army headed by **Field Marshal Sugiyama Hajime**. A graduate of the IJA military academy in 1900 and veteran of the Russo-Japanese War, his interwar period assignments included several attaché, League of Nations and aviation postings. He commanded the IJAAF, was War Minister during the Japanese occupation of Manchuria and led IJA forces in northern China and Mongolia in 1938. Sugiyama served as Chief of the Army General Staff from 1940 until February 1944. Tojo removed Sugiyama because of the army's failures in the Pacific to stop Allied advances, and reassigned him as inspector general for military education. Sugiyama became War Minister on 22 July 1944 after the Tojo government fell with Saipan's surrender. He became commander of the First General Army. Sugiyama's assignment included the defense of northern Honshu, which included the Kanto Plain area and Tokyo; IJA Headquarters took direct defense command of Hokkaido and the Kuril Islands. Even after the atomic bomb had been dropped on Hiroshima, Sugiyama continued to press for military operations against the Americans. He committed suicide after the end of the war.

The Imperial Japanese Navy (IJN) separated the command of fleet and shore establishments. By the war's end, the IJN had few remaining major surface vessels, but retained command of the Imperial Japanese Navy Air Force (IJNAF), small attack boats and various-sized submarines that could be used for suicide attacks. **Admiral Toyoda Soemu**, a 1905 graduate of the IJN's academy, was given control of the General Navy Command, which was responsible for several bases and facilities. He was elevated to command the Combined Fleet in May 1944. If the Americans invaded Japan, Toyoda would take charge of the few remaining surface vessels, and direct a sizable suicide force designed to strike at the American invasion forces. He would later argue to continue the war, despite the use of the atomic bombs. Admiral Toyoda was convicted of war crimes and was imprisoned from 1945 to 1948. Toyoda's insistence on a decisive battle ensured the limited IJN forces would evaporate further with destruction of carrier aircraft forces and surface forces.

OPPOSING PLANS

From mid-1944, Allied military operations had focused on defeating Germany first, limiting the allocation of resources to the struggle against Japanese forces. By September 1944, American and British forces had landed in northern and southern France, had advanced through Belgium and portions of the Netherlands, and were about to drive into Hitler's Germany. The war in Europe seemed to be in reach of conclusion. The focus began to turn to the Pacific, where the US Navy, Marine Corps and a sizable Army force had been fighting and pushing the Japanese back, supported by British, Chinese and Commonwealth military units pressurizing the Japanese in Burma.

Nimitz and MacArthur had embarked on major offensive pushes against the Japanese, which would deny Tokyo the ability to develop a defensive line or to conduct further major offensive operations. By September 1944, American forces had taken the Mariana Islands and were about to take the Philippines, thus moving closer to Japan. The capture of further island groups nearer to Japan would greatly increase the Allies' ability to unleash a strategic bombing campaign that could bring the war home to an enemy populace

From the opening years of the 20th century, American planners had formulated a strategy to defeat Japan in any eventual war. Part of War Plan Orange (the initial plan) emphasized the bombardment of cities, military targets, and in support of invasion operations. The USS *Iowa* was one of the ship that would be tasked with such missions. (DOD)

TOP, LEFT
US Navy submarine forces blockaded Japan effectively in 1945. Here the USS *Sea Dog's* crew searches for merchant ship targets in May. (DOD)

TOP, RIGHT
Japanese merchant shipping was at the mercy of American submarines, aircraft and surface ships. These ships were caught in Manila Bay. (DOD)

relatively untouched by direct attack. As American naval forces moved closer to Japan, the blockade and isolation of the home islands became more pronounced. Allied forces had conducted large-scale amphibious assaults and land campaigns in the Pacific before, but these were relatively short and intense battles – until the bloody campaign to take Okinawa in March 1945. The capture of the island forced Allied leadership to consider the next moves in bringing about Tokyo's surrender, while the Japanese leadership was now faced with a new and very real threat.

THE OPTIONS FOR JAPAN

By mid-1945, Japanese strategic command had few viable options to consider. Since her defeat at the Battle of Midway in June 1942, Japan's empire had gradually shrunk, and with it her economy and military capability. Although her armed forces could still fight, the top quality forces that had conquered the Pacific were gone. Tokyo had been forced to use suicide attacks by air and naval units. Germany had capitulated and now Japan was alone in facing the Allies. Japan had two options: attempt to negotiate a peace, or defend her empire to the bitter end.

Unless the Japanese government could secure certain pledges from the Allies, it would not surrender. The most important consideration was keeping the imperial system intact. The emperor's existence, symbolizing the essence of Japan, was the sticking point. Japan's acceptance of unconditional surrender terms would also dissolve their control of Manchuria and Southeast Asia, which would have severe economic and political ramifications. Allied forces would also dismantle the Japanese military, hold war crime tribunals and occupy the country. These conditions were unthinkable to many in Tokyo. However, some Japanese Foreign Ministry officials believed that the only option to stop the advancing American military tide was to start immediate negotiations for peace. At best this attempt might maintain the status quo to stop further contraction of Japanese dominion and control.

The Japanese prospects of regaining territory lost since 1942 were slim. American forces had advanced from the Marianas to the Ryukyu Islands and they could not be stopped. Japanese troops could certainly provide a spirited defense, but any opposition to full-scale American or Allied advance would inevitably be of limited duration and capability. One possible method of forcing a negotiated peace was by making the cost of American military actions very high in terms of casualties. Events on Okinawa in early 1945 had demonstrated that the tenacity and ferocity of the Japanese defense would only increase as America got closer to Tokyo. American forces took over three months to gain control of the island, suffering 72,358 killed, wounded and missing in the process. Estimates of Japanese military and civilian deaths ran at around 107,000. If Japan could make further casualties even greater for the Americans, then war weariness throughout the country could force Washington's hands to negotiate. Japan's leaders would not only employ the country's armed forces in any homeland military action, but also its civilian population.

THE ALLIED STRATEGY FOR VICTORY

Early in the war, US Navy leaders had continually demanded priority in the distribution of limited resources. The series of unchecked Japanese advances since Pearl Harbor had made the fight in the Pacific, rather than Europe, their main focus. The long-cherished vision of US naval commanders saw them winning the war against Japan. However, the US Army's focus, with the approval of Roosevelt, was to secure victory in Europe first. Brigadier General Thomas T. Handy, the chief US Army planner, played a particular role in proposing options other than naval victory in the Pacific for overcoming Japan. In 1942, Handy identified two options that would later become Truman's major strategic choices. American forces could use blockade and massive aerial bombardment to force Japan's capitulation; or, alternatively, an invasion could be launched to take over the country – essentially, attrition or direct action.

The B-29 was the ultimate strategic bomber, and destroyed many Japanese cities in numerous late-war raids. However, its development costs were very high – more than for the development of the first nuclear weapons. (US Air Force)

Engine malfunctions, poor bombing results, weather and other problems forced USAAF planners to re-think the B-29 operations. LeMay changed tactics to night, low-level and incendiary missions. (US Air Force)

Blockade and bombardment

Enforcing a blockade and using bombardment was not a new strategic approach to defeating Japan. Pre-World War II American naval strategy aimed at securing victory over Tokyo centered on a combination of blockade – to strangle Japan's industry, military and population into submission – followed by the exploitation of American naval superiority, with the Pacific Fleet defeating the Imperial Japanese Navy in a decisive battle. This framework to defeat Japan was known as War Plan Orange. From 1906 to 1941 various editions of this strategy were formalized. One major assumption contained within War Plan Orange was that the United States would receive little aid from other powers. War Plan Orange was incorporated into the subsequent Rainbow Plans. The revised Pacific plan consisted of three phases. The first phase would see Japanese forces overrunning "Blue" or American Pacific possessions (which would soon become reality). Phase II would see the American fightback, consisting of a combined US Navy and Army offensive effort to secure bases that would allow the Americans to sever Japanese lines of trade and communications. The third and final stage comprised a concentration on blockading Japanese ports and cutting supplies of food, raw materials, and other imports to force the country into submission; the US Pacific Fleet would also bombard Japanese coastal areas during this phase, which would continue until Tokyo surrendered. Naval planners saw the war in the Pacific as primarily a maritime conflict with little need for a large land campaign.

Senior US Navy officers had long been educated in this strategic plan, or indeed had been involved in its development. Given that the Pacific war began with events closely paralleling those forecasted in the Rainbow Plans, it is unsurprising that the top naval leadership advocated continuing to pursue the goals of the subsequent two phases, although how long it would take to force Japan's surrender was uncertain. The US Navy would drive through the Central Pacific, echoing the general outline of the plans, with its carrier capability adding pressure on Japan. American land forces would be required, however, to capture certain key islands in the Pacific for logistical reasons and to establish airfields to conduct strategic bombing missions by land-based aircraft. Extensive land campaigning to capture large tracts of land, such as the

Philippines, was unnecessary though. With Japanese naval power severely limited by the US Navy, her land forces in such locations would be starved of supplies or cut off. One drawback was that occupied native populations in the Pacific would continue to suffer Tokyo's oppressive rule.

The strategy of blockade did have some merit. The fact that Japan consisted of a collection of resource-poor islands, which were incapable of supporting her internal economy and of feeding her population, made the nation vulnerable to naval blockade. Allied submarines, surface vessels (especially minelayers) and aircraft could restrict naval traffic and cause great damage to vulnerable Japanese merchant shipping. In addition, once the

Japanese firefighting capability was supplemented by civilian efforts, as shown in this Japanese painting. Despite these efforts, B-29 incendiary bombing raids overwhelmed them. (US Army)

Japanese naval and air forces had been destroyed or diminished, American naval forces could tighten the noose around Japan even further. Before Pearl Harbor, Japan needed a merchant fleet of over 10,000,000 tons to supply iron ore, rubber, oil and food for the economy. The nation maintained a national merchant fleet of only 6,384,000 tons; the other required tonnage came from foreign sources. Loss of these foreign merchant ships as the war progressed meant Japan would face increasing problems as the war dragged on. Despite expanding its naval construction and pressing captured merchant shipping into service, Japanese oceanic transportation fell from 6,384,000 tons in December 1941 to 2,564,000 tons by the end of 1944. Allied, primarily American, submarines were responsible for sinking 4,313,101 tons of merchant ships, the leading cause of Japanese material losses: American submarine commanders sent more than 1,100 merchant ships to the ocean floor. By 1945, Allied submarines had put a chokehold on Japanese shipping trying to ply Japanese inter-island trade, and dominated the surrounding waters of the Japanese home islands.

The shrinkage in the Japanese merchant fleet had a catastrophic impact on her war economy, forcing Japanese officials to make tough choices between transferring military forces between the Asian mainland and Japan, importing natural resources, or making inter-coastal Japanese port calls to distribute products. Japanese imports of raw materials fell dramatically. Coal imports fell in 1945 to 7.3 percent of their 1941 level. Similarly, imports of iron ore were only at 2.6 percent and fertilizer at about 12.1 percent of the prewar acquisitions. Rubber fell from 31,818 tons to zero. Weapons production, electricity supplies and food production were severely restricted. It was clear that the American blockade was working, but this strategy required time, and to become more effective it required bases closer to the Japanese mainland in order to support naval and air operations.

The B-29 raids

Unlike the European Combined Bomber Offensive, in 1944 land-based strategic bombardment against Japan was a relatively new addition to the Pacific effort. The first bombing attack on Japan occurred on 18 April 1942

The 9/10 March 1945 firebombing of Tokyo

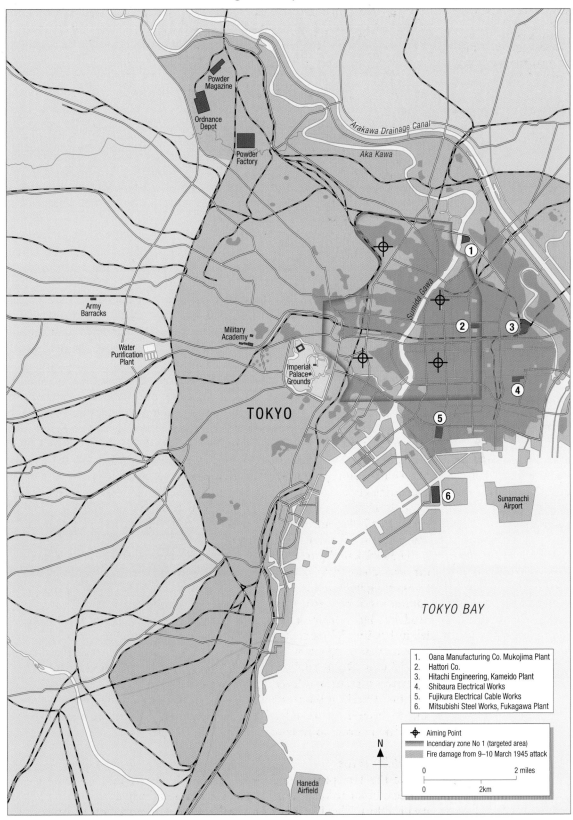

1. Oana Manufacturing Co. Mukojima Plant
2. Hattori Co.
3. Hitachi Engineering, Kameido Plant
4. Shibaura Electrical Works
5. Fujikura Electrical Cable Works
6. Mitsubishi Steel Works, Fukagawa Plant

Aiming Point
Incendiary zone No 1 (targeted area)
Fire damage from 9–10 March 1945 attack

0   2 miles
0   2km

with the Doolittle Raid, using land-based bombers launched from an aircraft carrier. This limited attack had a significant psychological impact on both America and Japan, but it did little in terms of physical damage. A sustained bombardment against Japan required appropriate airfields. In the European Combined Bomber Offensive, USAAF and Royal Air Force (RAF) aircraft used British bases to support B-17, B-24 and other aircraft in striking against key targets. The huge distances and variety of enemy dispositions in the Pacific required bases and airfields much nearer to the Japanese home islands. Additionally, a longer-range aircraft with a greater payload and which could fly faster and higher to escape enemy defenses than the B-17 and B-24 was required. The Boeing B-29 Superfortress was just such a plane. The B-29 could deliver 10 tons of bombs and had a combat radius of about 1,500 miles. USAAF officials had hoped that the B-29 would see service over Germany, but with priority given to the Pacific, air operations continued in Europe with existing aircraft types.

B-29 activities were kept under the control of the USAAF chief, General Henry "Hap" Arnold, with the establishment of the Twentieth Air Force. Arnold's motivation for taking responsibility for B-29 operations was that a unity of command was lacking in the Pacific: unlike in Europe, command of forces in the Pacific was split between Nimitz and MacArthur. Arnold wished to ensure a concentrated, decisive B-29 bombardment, and much was at stake with the B-29 operations. The program had been under pressure to produce results, partly owing to its $3 billion cost (the atomic bomb development expenses were about $2 billion), and the future role of USAAF and its organizational independence from the Army also depended on how this new aircraft performed. The B-29 wings also needed large airfields that would consume scarce building materials and engineering support in their development.

The first B-29 raids originated from Chengtu, an airfield in central China. During Operation *Matterhorn*, these Chinese-based B-29s struck the western edge of Kyushu, targeting coke ovens and an iron and steel works at Yawata

The fanatical defense of their homeland offered by Japanese soldiers and civilians might make an invasion extremely costly for US and Allied troops – a consideration not lost on these US Marines passing the body of a Japanese soldier on Okinawa in April 1945. (DOD)

on 15 June 1944, and parts of Manchuria. Despite hopes of great success from conventional, daylight precision B-29 attacks, the operational results were disappointing. Operation *Matterhorn* failed to destroy or significantly disrupt Japanese production activities in Kyushu or Manchuria. Poor logistics, problems with the B-29 engines, inclement weather, high-altitude winds and other issues all affected *Matterhorn*'s effectiveness. However, the results of the B-29 operations improved with the capture of bases in the Marianas and transfer of aircraft operations to these new locations. The US Navy was able to ship fuel, spare parts and other essential supplies to bases on Saipan, Tinian and Guam, which allowed B-29 bombing raids on Japan to achieve much greater effectiveness. One other drawback of the Chinese bases was that they were vulnerable to capture or disruption by Japanese land forces or air attack. Both the presence of the American Pacific Fleet and the distances between the island bases afforded them protection from land invasion, naval strikes and air attack. The Marianas bases allowed the USAAF B-29s to be in range of major economic, military and political centers like Tokyo, Kobe, Osaka and Nagoya. Weather conditions for take-off and landings were also better in these locations.

Flying operations from these new bomber bases commenced against Tokyo on 24 November 1944. However, bombing results remained disappointing. USAAF doctrine had focused on high-altitude, high-explosive daylight, precision targeting against specific military and economic centers,

THE TOKYO FIREBOMBING RAID (pp. 26–27)

The massive 9/10 March 1945 night attack on Tokyo was a devastating message sent to the Japanese government and people by the USAAF that the war had reached a new level. Curtis LeMay ordered 334 aircraft to attack Tokyo at night. 279 B-29s arrived over the area to deliver incendiary low-level bombing, which resulted in casualties estimated somewhere between 96,000 and 197,000. *Dauntless Dotty* **(1)**, from the 869th Bombardment Squadron, was piloted by Robert Morgan. Morgan had gained earlier fame as commander of the first USAAF B-17 crew to complete 25 combat missions in Europe flying the *Memphis Belle*. LeMay had allowed his pilots to attack the city at various altitudes and individually, not in formation, which confused the defenses. B-29s, like *Dauntless Dotty* or *American Made* **(2)**, carried six to eight tons of bundled M-69 incendiary bombs **(3)**. Each B-29 could carry more bombs and fuel since LeMay ordered the removal of all defensive armament, their crews and ammunition, except for the tail guns. About 16 square miles of Tokyo were destroyed by the firestorm **(4)**. On this night, USAAF crews suffered no reported losses to fighters, and only 14 B-29s were lost; overall, 42 aircraft were damaged by flak. The Japanese were completely surprised by the change in bombing tactics and their defenses proved inadequate, since their primary means to detect the night-raiding B-29s was by using searchlights. Ground radar units had detected some of the bombers, but could not pinpoint their targets. As the firestorm grew, the Japanese searchlight and flak capability diminished as equipment and crews were overcome by fire and heat. Morgan completed another 25 combat missions in the Pacific before returning home in April 1945.

such as the Japanese aircraft industry, urban industrial areas and enemy shipping. Major General Curtis E. LeMay replaced Major General Haywood S. Hansell, Jr of the XXI Bomber Command part of Twentieth Air Force. The new command was now responsible for B-29 operations in the central Pacific. Enemy air defenses were not a problem, the quantity and quality of Japanese interceptor and antiaircraft defenses was shrinking. Pressure to improve the results forced a drastic change in tactics, which in turn would alter the broader strategy. LeMay switched to low-altitude, incendiary night attacks against urban areas in the wake of frustration about poor, high-altitude, precision strike effects, mirroring the RAF's efforts in the Combined Bomber Offensive. Japanese use of wood and paper in construction, the congested nature of their industrial areas, the dispersal of industry and other factors led to US bombers switching to incendiary devices. The devastating raids that resulted did not distinguish between military or civilian targets.

On the night of 9/10 March 1945, LeMay unleashed a ruinous attack against Tokyo. The raid was arguably the most effective one launched in the course of the whole war against a Japanese city, even taking into account the atomic bomb attacks on Hiroshima and Nagasaki. The 279-plane raid exceeded expectations. LeMay staggered his B-29 bombers at altitudes ranging from 4,900 to 9,200ft – as opposed to the typical 30,000ft daylight altitudes – and 1,665 tons of incendiaries were dropped. Weather conditions created a firestorm that reached heights of 2,000ft and was visible 150 miles away. The B-29 aircrews escaped unscathed, but Tokyo's population suffered between 72,489 and 83,793 deaths, and some 1 million people were made homeless. Some estimates put casualties as high as 197,000 killed and missing. Over 16 square miles of the city were burned out. LeMay would repeat the incendiary raid on Osaka, Nagoya and Kobe within 10 days. Aerial bombardment had proved itself to be a powerful tool with which to hammer Japan.

Carrier raids

Increasing Allied naval strength and the reduction of the Imperial Japanese Navy allowed the United States and Great Britain to add another dimension to the strategic calculus: carrier-borne aircraft raids on Japan, particularly after Okinawa had been secured. On 10 July 1945, Task Force 38, under Marc A. Mitscher, conducted a series of attacks on airfields around Tokyo. Perhaps because of the limited strength of the IJAAF and IJNAF or attempts to hoard aircraft for suicide missions, Mitscher and others could freely sail around Japanese waters with impunity from attack by enemy aircraft. Task Force 37, with 105 US Navy and 28 Royal Navy vessels, was created on 17 July 1945. These combined forces could call upon at least 1,000 US Navy and Marine Corps aircraft and over 244 Royal Navy planes.

It was hoped that day- and night-bombing raids might bring Japan to her knees; LeMay estimated that he would force Tokyo to surrender by 1 October. If the United States could capture bases closer to Japan, B-17 and B-24 aircraft could add their weight to the campaign too. However, critics of the bombardment option pointed out that the extensive Combined Bomber Offensive campaign alone did not defeat Germany. Additionally, Secretary of War Stimson was concerned about continued bombing attacks against urban areas. In his 6 June 1945 diary entry, he expressed his fears that the United States might earn the "reputation of outdoing Hitler in atrocities" if raids like the Tokyo 9/10 March attack continued. Also, the bombardment option might take years to bring about the desired result.

The 9/10 March 1945 incendiary attack on Tokyo added new pressures on the Japanese. The USAAF used 279 B-29s to bomb the Asakusa/Sumida area. (US Air Force)

Invasion and occupation

American Army and Navy planners started to focus on another way to achieve Japan's capitulation: invasion and occupation. During the Casablanca Conference in January 1943, Roosevelt had announced an unconditional surrender policy. This guiding principle would rally public support for the war and demonstrate commitment to Moscow in the war against Germany. This policy would also force other Allied governments and the American people to accept nothing less from Tokyo. This political requirement of forcing Japan to unconditionally surrender affected the invasion planning process. Amphibious assaults on enemy territory were well-worn, albeit bloody, paths to victory in the Pacific. Allied forces had extensive experience of planning, supporting and executing large-scale, amphibious invasions, as demonstrated in North Africa, Sicily, France and operations throughout the Southwest and Central Pacific. A Japanese home island invasion seemed a logical extension of the current advance. The US War Department's Operations Plans Division (OPD) saw blockade and aerial bombardment as unsatisfactory as early as April 1944. Japan's fall, according to Army OPD planners, could only come from an invasion of the home islands.

Despite growing doubts from Navy planners, the American Joint War Plans Committee (JWPC) created an initial concept of attacking Japan. However, problems quickly arose. Given the fanatical Japanese resistance, a home island invasion would require massive forces and might result in many casualties. Unconditional surrender might mean the end of the imperial monarchy, sustained occupation and the loss of territory. Surrender was an alien concept: Japan had never been successfully invaded or occupied. Another constraint was the American and British agreement to force the surrender of Japan within 12 months of Germany's fall.

Logistics would also be a problem for any invasion. American military forces would require extensive supply, transportation and maintenance resources to avert Japanese starvation and social collapse. Another major problem was the lack of detailed information about Japanese homeland defenses. American intelligence officials relied on intercepted radio signals based on MAGIC (diplomatic) and ULTRA (military) decrypted Japanese

The USAAF tried to use B-29 raids in a daylight precision-bombing role. Unfortunately meteorological conditions, the limited range of the bombers and other issues forced Curtis LeMay to switch to incendiary night raids, which proved devastating, as shown here. (US Air Force).

dispatches. American forces did not have access to detailed aerial photography, nor were there spies or knowledgeable individuals present in the country to pass on appropriate information.

Heavy casualties at Iwo Jima and Okinawa forced military and national leaders, especially Truman, to reconsider an invasion's cost and the impact on public support. British, Commonwealth and other Allied support for the invasion was mixed. Britain was drained militarily and economically after defeating Germany. European military forces were clamoring for demobilization. Either this would create problems during any redeployment of such war-weary troops, or else the demobilized veterans would be replaced by inexperienced troops, prone to making mistakes or buckling under pressure in any future Okinawa-style battle. Despite this, the Allied nations did want to participate in an invasion, although they would require time to train, redeploy, equip and reorganize themselves.

The JWPC concept was modified over time and resulted in a preliminary plan being ready on 5 May 1945. The final invasion concept consisted of Operation *Downfall*, which was developed by MacArthur's staff. This would see an initial extensive use of air and naval blockade, aerial bombardment and then a two-phase invasion (operations *Olympic* and *Coronet*), the details of which will be covered later.

DIPLOMACY OR DESTRUCTION

Another option that was available to both sides was a diplomatic solution. Since Pearl Harbor, the United States and Japan had broken off all forms of diplomatic contact. The only international power that might support this effort was the Soviet Union. For their part, Japanese diplomats might be able to persuade the Soviet government to broker a negotiated settlement between themselves and the Allies. Japan could provide territorial concessions in exchange. A major assumption of theirs was that Moscow would support such an effort. However, if Japan stood at the doors of defeat, the Soviets might simply declare war on her and enjoy greater territorial gain than might result from a political settlement.

From a US perspective, a negotiated peace was not sought by the majority of the war cabinet, especially following the call for the Axis powers to unconditionally surrender. Although some US War and State Department officials sought ways to get Japan to surrender without an invasion, the unconditional surrender policy hindered their attempts. A retreat from unconditional surrender might be seen as a softening of Washington's support for further military operations and could embolden the Japanese further. Conversely, getting Moscow to finally declare war against Japan might be sufficiently shocking to force Tokyo to surrender. Soviet forces could also hold down Japanese military units in China, Manchuria and Korea, forcing Japan to fight on a new front. Long-term negotiations between Washington, London and Moscow, dating back to the Tehran Conference in November 1943, had paid dividends to Truman as Josef Stalin agreed to move forces east to fight Japan after Germany's surrender. US leaders chose to ignore their concerns about postwar Soviet expansion in Asia, and territorial concessions.

MAGIC intercepts allowed Washington to discover that Japanese diplomats had sought out Moscow to act as their intermediary for a negotiated peace with Washington. However, the Soviets were readying to attack Japan, in line with the agreements reached among the Allies at the February 1945 Yalta Conference. In late July 1945, Truman, Churchill and Stalin met at Potsdam, Germany to discuss a number of issues to include Japan. During the conference, Truman sought and received Stalin's final assurance of entering the war, on 9 August.

Washington had one final, but as yet untested, option: the atomic bomb. Most military leaders had agreed that Japan's military and economy was already weakened and Tokyo's surrender was imminent. Persuading a virtually defeated enemy to surrender might require an act of significant shock. A Soviet war declaration might suffice, but so could Washington's use of the atomic bomb.

The US Army had begun its project to build an atomic bomb on 16 August 1942, under the auspices of the Manhattan Project (also sometimes referred to as the Manhattan Engineering District). Under the direction of Major General Leslie R. Groves, the project grew in size to comprise a design center at Los Alamos and two work centers at Hanford, Washington and Clinton, Tennessee. By August 1945, the teams at Los Alamos, New Mexico had succeeded in designing, developing and building a gun-type atomic bomb that would force five pounds of uranium-235 against another 17 pounds at high speed; this would create critical mass and release tremendous heat, light, blast and radiation effects. Groves and the Manhattan Project personnel believed that this bomb did not need an operational test. The team was also experimenting with an even greater device, the plutonium bomb, which would require testing before use. Each of the atomic weapons had the capability to destroy an entire city on its own. Some Army and USAAF officials saw the atomic bomb as nothing more than a convenient replacement for the massive incendiary B-29 raids under way against Japan, where one bomber could take the place of hundreds of these missions.

Although President Roosevelt knew that the Manhattan Project was proceeding, the then Vice President Truman did not, and Truman was informed about the bomb only after becoming president. Stimson first briefed

Truman on 12 April about the new weapons. Groves and Stimson later told Truman that within four months "the most terrible weapon ever known to human history, one bomb of which could destroy a whole city" would be available. These weapons also had delivery systems, modified B-29 Superfortresses assigned to a special unit, the 509th Composite Group. Despite arguments by some scientists, engineers and government officials about the moral justification for the destruction of an entire city by a single nuclear weapon, the United States had already begun incendiary attacks on major Japanese cities, resulting in tens of thousands of civilian deaths. Many senior Roosevelt administration officials had started, well before Truman's presidency, to think about the use of an atomic bomb against Germany. In many ways, the acceptance of using the atomic bomb had already been made; the only consideration was when the Manhattan Project personnel could perfect the weapon.

Although developed too late to use against Germany, the uranium and plutonium bombs could still be dropped on Japan. However, by early August 1945, scientists had managed to produce sufficient nuclear material to build only a single uranium device, Little Boy, and a plutonium bomb, Fat Man. They might not have enough material to build another bomb if the first uses failed to bring about the required strategic results. This was yet another factor that made the strategic decision-making process even more difficult for the US leadership.

OPERATION *DOWNFALL*: THE INVASION OF JAPAN

By the end of March 1945, the top American leaders had decided to continue with the plan to invade Japan. Admiral King, never an invasion fan, believed that Fleet Admiral Chester W. Nimitz and Supreme Commander of Allied Forces in the Southwest Pacific Area General Douglas MacArthur should continue their build-up and planning efforts, but held that the decision to launch Operation *Downfall* was not irrevocable. Attacks could continue against Japan's periphery whilst any direct attack could be set aside. Fleet Admiral William D. Leahy (Truman's chief of staff) also sought a reprieve from the invasion drumbeat, fearing the expected heavy casualties. General of the Army George C. Marshall held a contrary opinion, believing that Truman had approved the start of preparations to take Kyushu. The Joint Chiefs of Staff directed MacArthur and Nimitz to present them with an attack plan.

PHASE ONE: OPERATION *OLYMPIC*

The first phase of Operation *Downfall* would comprise Operation *Olympic*, the main aims of which were to seize southern Kyushu for air and naval bases

Japanese military logistics and transportation were at ever increasing risk from growing American air and naval strength. This ammunition train would provide a ripe target. (US Army)

Planned Operation *Olympic* invasion sites on Kyushu

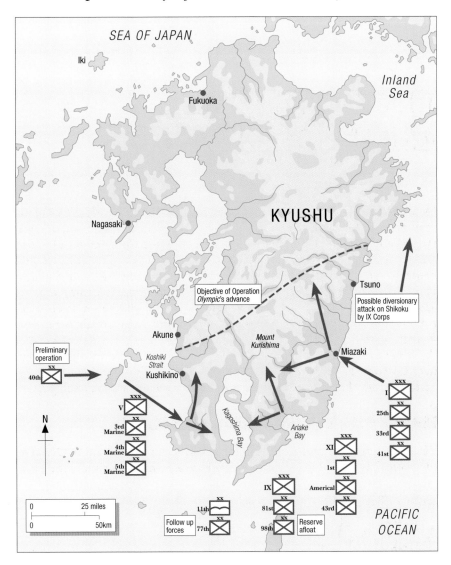

to enhance attacks on Japan's main island, Honshu. MacArthur's Sixth Army, under General Walter Krueger, would plan and lead the Kyushu invasion. Krueger would use nine Army and three Marine Corps divisions in the initial assault. Two Army divisions would provide follow-up capability. Krueger could rely on two reserve divisions in the Philippines and one in the Ryukus.

MacArthur's staff had several options for where the invasion fleet could land: within Kagoshima Bay, the western side of Kyushu bordering the Koshiki Strait up to Kushikino, Ariake Bay, or on Kyushu's eastern coast near Miazaki. Mountain ranges ringed each of these potential landing sites. The geography of the locations was the determining factor in the final choice of the invasion site. Army officers rejected the long and narrow Kagoshima Bay: Krueger's force could be swallowed up by a concentrated suicide attack and trapped. The other sites offered a wider and less risky approach. MacArthur decided to split his forces and use all of the other three landing sites. On the day of the invasion, or X-Day, the American forces would land and then push

through the limited number of mountain passes and then drive northwards. Once American units had cleared southern Kyushu, American engineers could build airfields and use Kagoshima Bay as a major naval base and port for further operations against the largest of the Japanese home islands, Honshu.

On X-4 (i.e. four days before X-Day), the US 40th Infantry Division with the 158th Regimental Combat Team would conduct preliminary operations to take the islands off Kyushu. This would provide some close support bases to help the invasion. Additionally, the 81st and 98th Infantry divisions would conduct a feint by landing on Shikoku on X-2. These units also served as floating reserve forces. USAAF officials in the Pacific projected that they would need between 14 and 17 American divisions to control southern

Kyushu. American invasion forces, once they could consolidate their invasion sites, would drive north to push towards a line running from Sendai on the western coast to Tsuno.

PHASE TWO: OPERATION *CORONET*

If the Japanese did not surrender after Operation *Olympic*, then the Allies would conduct an invasion of Honshu via the Kanto Plain (Operation *Coronet*). This attack, aimed at Tokyo and the industrial heart of the nation, would deliver a "knock-out blow." MacArthur would lead the Honshu assault with the First and Eighth Armies composed of nine infantry and three US Marine Corps divisions. After the initial amphibious landings, a force of three infantry and one Marine divisions and two armoured divisions would come ashore. After 90 days, MacArthur's staff assumed that the presence of four divisions would be required to support operations, rotating as required.

The concept of Operation *Coronet* called for invasion at two sites on the eastern coast of central Honshu. Allied military forces would drive to envelop the Tokyo and Yokohama urban areas and the remainder of the Kanto Plain. MacArthur's planners believed up to 25 divisions would be needed to seize all the objectives. American units were earmarked for the initial invasion forces and reinforcements, but MacArthur would call upon Australian, British, Canadian and French divisions for subsequent operations if Japanese resistance did not collapse. The plans also included possible advances into southern Shikoku (the smallest of the four home islands) and southeast Honshu to establish airfields, vital for gaining air superiority as well as for close air support and interdiction missions.

Japanese defenders in Okinawa used well-prepared defensive positions to inflict heavy casualties on the invading forces. These US Marines have used dynamite to destroy a cave used by Japanese troops. Future operations on the home islands might require similar tactics. (DOD)

Planned Operation *Coronet* invasion sites on Honshu

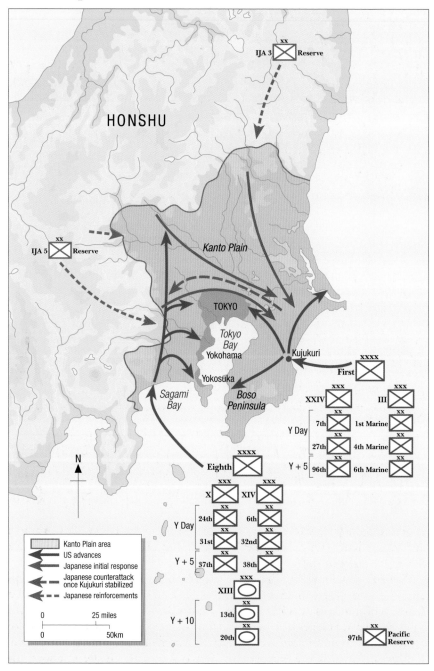

The main thrust into the Kanto Plain was reserved for the Eighth Army under Lieutenant General Robert L. Eichelberger. His forces would land in Sagami Bay. On the day of the invasion (Y-Day), the Eighth Army divisions would drive directly north to isolate major urban areas and seize territory. The initial invasion force consisted of four infantry divisions that would advance against targets on the eastern shore of Tokyo Bay. Advancing from the west, these infantry divisions could capture the IJN base at Yokosuka, the Yokohama industrial center and Tokyo. Five days after the invasion,

reinforcements from two infantry divisions would come ashore. Two armored divisions, which would land 10 days after Y-Day, would drive north to block the approach of any IJA reinforcements.

Redeployed American divisions from Europe and some Marine Corps divisions were placed under the control of General Courtney H. Hodges' First Army. These forces would land less than 40 miles east of Tokyo on the Kujukuri coast. Hodges had a less ambitious, but key mission. Plans called for his divisions to drive northwest to support Eichelberger's attack on Tokyo, southwest towards the entrance to Tokyo Bay, and northeast above the invasion site. An Army infantry division and Marine division would reinforce Hodges' forces five days after the invasion.

Marshall and MacArthur also explored the use of chemical weapons for Operation *Downfall* in an effort to reduce American casualties. These could be especially effective against Japanese troops entrenched in caves and in beach defensive emplacements; such defenses were time-consuming to clear and were responsible for heavy American casualties. The threat of retaliation in kind with the use of Japanese chemical and biological weapons, which had been used in China, forced US planners to set their use aside.

America's ability to supply Pacific forces assured Washington it could cope with any invasion of Japan. These Liberty ships would ensure sufficient transports were available to supply American logistical requirements. (DOD)

SETTING A TIMEFRAME

On 3 April 1945, the US Joint Chiefs of Staff's invasion guidance indicated that Operation *Olympic* would begin on 1 December 1945 and with the follow-on Operation *Coronet*, if required, beginning on 1 March 1946. However, the Washington planners had ignored the local weather conditions for the December amphibious operations. Low cloud and poor visibility could hamper aerial operations, whilst the rain, wind and cold would affect landing activities and maneuvering across territory crisscrossed with rivers and streams. Fortunately, this was not lost on MacArthur's and Nimitz's staffs. The only options were to move *Olympic* to March 1946, or to start the invasion earlier. If the invasion began in March 1946, then the end of the war would have to be delayed beyond the agreed 12 months after Germany's surrender. If Washington moved it forward, then logistical and force organizational problems had to be resolved. On 24 April 1945, after comparing all options, the US Joint Chiefs of Staff came to the conclusion that only an invasion could force Japan's unconditional surrender. On 25 May, they rescheduled the start date for *Olympic* to 1 November 1945.

In the early summer of 1945, little was known about the quality of enemy opposition. ULTRA intercepts could provide information on troop movements, but nothing detailed on enemy strategic intentions. Planning for the attack on Japan by amphibious assault, as well as the number of likely Allied casualties that would result, was thus based on a series of assumptions about Tokyo's ability to reinforce and defend the initial objective of Kyushu.

American analysts estimated that two IJA combat divisions, an independent tank regiment and two depot divisions (these had equipment and cadre, but not sufficient assigned combat personnel) were present on Kyushu on 12 May 1945. They further estimated that by 1 November 1945 the IJA would have three combat divisions in southern Kyushu and some other smaller units. In northern Kyushu, Tokyo would probably be guarded by three combat divisions and as well as depot divisions, forces primarily transferred from Manchuria and Honshu. The total enemy strength would not exceed 350,000 soldiers, sailors and airmen by 1 November, in contrast to the current 246,000 deployed.

Unfortunately for US planners, estimates of enemy forces moving into Kyushu, especially near the planned southern invasion sites, started to rise significantly. By 16 June, current troop strength estimates on Kyushu, gleaned from ULTRA intercepts, topped 300,000. By 2 August it had mushroomed to 534,000, compared with a projected 766,700-strong US invasion force. Japanese mobilized civilians could also replace IJA uniformed logistics and support personnel, thus releasing more of them for combat duty. ULTRA decrypted messages indicated that the Japanese had a large inventory of 3,335 combat and 3,530 training aircraft, albeit obsolete, which could be used for kamikaze attacks. These aircraft only needed limited fuel and basic pilot skills for their one-way missions. Allied photographic intelligence supported the ULTRA-derived claims. Nimitz's intelligence staff estimated that 10,290 aircraft were available on 13 August for Japanese homeland defense.

Okinawa saw the first use of massed kamikaze attacks. Japanese Army and Navy kamikaze special air attack units had launched about 1,900 sorties, causing 4,907 US Navy deaths and netting 35 ships sunk and 137 vessels damaged. Combined with similar losses earlier in the Philippines, kamikazes had sunk 57 ships, and 100 out of 300 attacked ships had suffered sufficient damage to have them withdrawn from service. A direct amphibious assault on Japan would see an even greater kamikaze effort, with suicide attacks on the invasion fleet. If a kamikaze pilot took off, he had a 32 percent chance of hitting a ship – a success rate 700 to 1,000 percent greater than conventional aircraft attack.

Despite ULTRA information, MacArthur's *Olympic* planners did not know the specific plans of the Japanese defenders. MacArthur's G-2 staff had surmised that "troop movements and dispositions clearly emphasize preparation for all-out defense of the home islands" and that Tokyo considered invasion "certain if not imminent." However, questions remained over the composition, location, strength, employment and nature of the Japanese defenders. MacArthur's G-2, Major General Charles A. Willoughby, had consistently downplayed the ULTRA reports, as he had done for Japanese force strengths throughout the Pacific campaign. ULTRA intercepts indicated that Tokyo had built beach defenses where the invading US Sixth Army would land. Additionally, G-2 officials began to fear the Japanese might employ "chemical or new kinds of weapons."

Tough fighting was forecast for the troops involved in Operation *Downfall*. These US Marines in Okinawa were well prepared, though, having fought a prolonged and bloody campaign there between March and June 1945. (DOD)

The severe casualties suffered at Okinawa demonstrated Japanese determination not to surrender. President Truman was very concerned that a Kyushu invasion would be nothing more than an expanded version of Okinawa, which in turn would be dwarfed by future Honshu operations. If the original Operation *Downfall* option were exercised, a 15 June 1945 JWPC study speculated, American casualties would reach 193,500. If the Allies managed to occupy northern Kyushu, the casualties would then rise to 220,000. Marshall, concerned about Truman's casualty fears, asked MacArthur for an estimate. His staff believed 105,050 Americans would be killed, wounded or missing within 90 days. MacArthur downplayed the study after Marshall questioned him over it. MacArthur thought casualties would be similar to Luzon, in the Philippines, for the first 30 days at around 31,000. *Olympic*'s main objective, to seize southern Kyushu, however, was only a warm-up for *Coronet*.

Discussions about casualties became the key point when Truman met Henry Stimson (head of the War Department), Marshall, Fleet Admiral Ernest King, Leahy and several others on 18 June 1945. Marshall presented the various casualty reports and concluded that losses would resemble Luzon. Leahy countered that it would repeat the Okinawa experience with a 35 percent American casualty rate or more. Using the number of American forces planned for *Olympic*, the total would run well over 268,000. During the meeting, Marshall claimed that air and naval forces could bring effective results by continuing the blockade and pummeling of Japanese forces. Prior discussions about blockade and bombardment had concluded that the option would take too long and would extend the war, but Marshall curiously now claimed they could work quickly. Reluctantly, Truman's only choice was to give tentative approval for *Olympic*, with approval of the final invasion orders to follow later. The day before, Truman had agonized over his decision in his diary entry, writing: "I have to decide Japanese strategy – shall we invade Japan proper or shall we bomb and blockade? That is my hardest decision to date. But I'll make it when I have all the facts." He did not mention the atomic bomb.

THE JAPANESE RESPONSE

The continued naval blockade, intensified aerial bombardment, attrition of forces, American advance towards Japan and increased attention by the Allies seemed to point towards Tokyo's military defeat. However, the Japanese government seemed determined not to allow its empire to dissolve. Since 1942, Japanese military planners had seen their isolated Pacific outposts bypassed or taken by growing Allied military might. Japan's strategic defensive perimeter had begun to disappear as the Philippines, Iwo Jima and Okinawa fell. The only question that the Imperial General Headquarters staff pondered was whether the Americans would launch their invasion on Kyushu or directly on Honshu. Emperor Hirohito had approved the "Outline of Army and Navy Operations" on 20 January 1945, which would become the basis for future homeland defense. The plan focused on defensive preparations on Japanese-held territory and kept the focus on inflicting attritional losses that would affect the American will to fight. The plan's authors placed their defensive attention on southern Kyushu and the Kanto Plain around Tokyo. By 26 February, War Ministry and Army commanders intended to mobilize up to 42 divisions and 18 independent brigades composed of over 1.5 million troops for homeland defense.

Kamikaze aircraft would make any invasion costly for the Americans. The IJNAF and IJAAF hoped to repeat the devastating damage inflicted in their attack on the USS *Bunker Hill* on 11 May 1945, where 389 crewmen lost their lives following two kamikaze hits. (DOD)

The IJA's Sixth Air Army and the IJN's Fifth Air Fleet would have the primary role of hitting hard at the American invasion fleet with a massive air counterattack. Along with elements from the First Air Army, Fifth Air Army, Third Air Fleet and Tenth Air Fleet, the focus would be on strikes aimed at the US carriers (330 IJNAF aircraft were assigned to this task), gunnery ships (250 IJAAF and IJNAF aircraft assigned) and transports (which would be targeted by 24-hour-a-day suicide attacks for 10 days). Trainers, transports, float planes, bombers and obsolete fighters would serve as kamikazes, and the air attacks on the transports would also involve all available aircraft not assigned to other duties. Although Japanese fighters could do little to stem B-29 raids anyway, they could make an invasion fleet suffer. Of course, IJAAF and IJNAF fighters would have to achieve air superiority over these areas first, which was a questionable assumption in the face of US air strength. *Kaiten* suicide midget submarines and other special attack units would also target any invasion fleet. Suicide attacks were vital to the effort. Imperial General Headquarters hoped that their suicide, or *tokko*, units would cause a 30–40 percent loss to the invasion fleet. After Okinawa, IJN officials raised the loss estimate to 30–50 percent. *Tokko* units, they believed, could make a major difference.

IJA field commanders received detailed instructions on 8 April to conduct homeland defense preparations. The *Ketsu-Go* Operation divided the empire into seven areas, with strategic emphasis on Kyushu and the Kanto Plain. Japanese military planning assumed American amphibious forces could not be stopped on the beaches with the few forces available. Instead, Japanese defenders would concentrate near the predicted invasion beaches and then strike American units before they could consolidate their positions. Fixed defenses could slow the Americans, but a mobile defense reserve could force a bloody confrontation. Creating massed casualties was a goal to demonstrate Japanese resolve to fight to the end and perhaps discourage further operations.

Following the fall of Okinawa, Japanese military planners predicted that the next stop would be Kyushu. The Japanese strategic planners selected the same beaches picked by MacArthur's staff for Operation *Olympic* as the most likely sites for any landings. By July 1945, IJA and IJN staffs had intended to concentrate their forces on the Ariake Bay and Miazaki areas. IJA planners concentrated their *Ketsu-Go* operations on southern Kyushu since they thought the possibility of landings farther north was a remote one. The danger of selectively defending Ariake Bay and Miazaki was that they would allow American divisions to consolidate their positions at other landing sites and crush them in a vise-like maneuver. Hata's Second General Army officers also foresaw Kyushu as being an American objective to gain bases for their air and naval forces. He also believed airborne operations against Kyushu and a simultaneous landing on southern Shikoku were likely.

The Fifty-Seventh Army defended the area around Ariake Bay and Miyazaki. The 86th Division was stationed at Ariake Bay, while the 154th and 156th divisions watched the Miazaki coastal areas. Hata's mobile reserves would be based near Mount Kurishima with at least five divisions and several independent brigades. They would move against the enemy with all available forces. The poor quality of the roads, the few passes, and a lack of motorized and rail transportation would limit their ability to hit American units in these areas, though. As a result, Japanese forces would have to move quickly and forecast correctly where to fight a "decisive" battle for Kyushu.

In terms of the Japanese defensive planning for an Allied invasion on the Kanto Plain (against Operation *Coronet*), the IJA and IJN staffs had hoped that a bloody defense of Kyushu might deter the Americans from a similar effort on Honshu. Japanese government officials gave defensive preparations for Kyushu a higher priority than ones on Honshu. Japanese air attacks could provide a way to reduce the American invasion fleet. However, the IJA and IJN suicide and special-attack forces might be used up in Kyushu's defense.

The IJA's First General Army had overall responsibility for the Kanto Plain ground defense. Homeland defense plans suggested Kujukuri was the primary target with a secondary one of Sagami Bay. Fifteen IJA divisions defended the Kujukuri beaches and five divisions were located at Sagami Bay. Owing to the critical nature of the Kanto Plain and the lack of strategic depth, IJA forces had to defend every square foot of land. By July 1945, the IJA had 11 combat divisions, two armoured divisions, seven coastal combat divisions, seven independent mixed brigades and three armoured brigades. These forces seemed formidable, but the armament, equipage and logistical support for the Second General Army on Kyushu became the primary focus for combat readiness.

THE APPROACH TO ARMAGEDDON

J. Robert Oppenheimer was the chief civilian scientific adviser to the Manhattan Project. He pushed for the bomb's operational use. (National Archives)

In early March 1945, Secretary of War Henry L. Stimson had begun to give serious thought to using the atomic bomb to avoid an invasion of Japan and to end the war quickly. Along with Joseph C. Grew, former US Ambassador to Japan, Stimson tried to persuade the Truman administration to remove the unconditional surrender terms in order to get Japan to lay down its arms. The United States could allow the emperor to stay on the throne, which would help ease the transition of government and allow a host of changes to Japan. Stimson's fear was that, without the emperor to direct the Japanese people and ensure adherence to new Allied policies, chaos could result in the country. Opponents bristled at the idea of letting the emperor survive, since to them this smacked of appeasement and might embolden the Japanese to fight on. Many senior State Department officials echoed public sentiment that Hirohito was equivalent to Hitler. As a result, Stimson's efforts failed.

THE CHOICE OF TARGET

On 5 March Stimson held discussions with George C. Marshall in which it was stated that the United States would soon decide whether to use the new atomic weapons. In anticipation of their deployment, Marshall directed Major General Leslie R. Groves (the military director of the Manhattan Project) to form a Targeting Committee to examine where to drop the atomic bombs. Starting work on 27 April, the committee, composed of Manhattan Project and USAAF personnel, met at Los Alamos and discussed how to maximize the impact of any use of the atomic bomb, aiming to show the Japanese government how it would bring great devastation. The Allied incendiary bombing missions had already severely damaged several large Japanese cities, with thousands of civilians incinerated.

Grove's Targeting Committee used several criteria to choose sites. The target had to have strategic value to the Japanese and be located between Tokyo and Nagasaki; the target had to have a large urban area at least three miles in diameter; and it had to be relatively untouched by previous USAAF bombings – ironically spared for potential atomic destruction at a later date. Another key condition was that, as far as could be ascertained, the areas should contain no Allied prisoner of war concentrations. Unfortunately, with little information about prisoner locations, this stipulation was difficult to predict with any accuracy. After considering 17 candidates, the committee initially selected five targets: Hiroshima, Yokohama, Kokura, Niigata and Kyoto. On 28 May, committee members reduced the candidates to Kyoto,

Niigata and Hiroshima. Hiroshima contained Hata's Second General Army headquarters and a large shipyard. Niigata was a huge industrial city and contained a port. Kyoto had significant cultural and religious importance for the Japanese. Stimson, who had warned Arnold about the impact on the civilian population of targeting cities with incendiary attacks, removed Kyoto from the list after heated arguments with Groves. On 21 July, Truman agreed with Stimson, while in Potsdam, that Kyoto should be spared. Kokura, the site of a large arsenal and ordnance works, replaced it on the list, but LeMay's staff purportedly added Nagasaki as an alternate target in case of weather concerns: its Mitsubishi arms, electric and ordnance factories and dockyards provided a lucrative target.

Depending on the weather conditions, one of the four targets would be hit. Hiroshima was marked down as the primary target; American planners did not know the city held 23 Allied prisoners of war. The Manhattan Project's top scientist, Dr. J. Robert Oppenheimer, helped the Targeting Committee by examining specific technical and operating issues related to the atomic bomb's use, including the height of detonation, radiological effects, safety requirements and other factors.

While the Target Committee examined the sites to be bombed, a top-level civilian Interim Committee was formed to examine and advise on how to use the bomb. Stimson chaired this committee, which met for the first time on 9 May. Some dissent was heard from Manhattan scientists and engineers about using the "gadget" on a target during these meetings, arguing the weapon might not work and that the Japanese might position prisoners of war on the sites. A further factor raised was that Manhattan Project personnel would be able to produce sufficient nuclear material only for the Little Boy uranium

B-29s were not the only aircraft to strike Japan in 1945. Carrier-based aircraft, like these TBM Avenger bombers and SB2C Helldivers, hit targets throughout coastal Japan. (DOD)

Throughout Kyushu and Honshu, the emperor had ordered defense emplacements to be built to counter an imminent American amphibious invasion. This sketch shows an emplacement at Sagami Bay on Honshu, one of the proposed invasion sites. (US Army)

bomb and the Fat Man plutonium bomb by early August. However, the committee members could find no other practical alternative than to drop the atomic bomb and on 1 June, they recommended that Truman use the weapons. Stimson relayed the committee's recommendation to Truman in a 6 June meeting. Stimson remarked that using the atomic bombs would be no worse than the current incendiary bombing missions over Japan and that it might not be of as great a shock value as initially thought. The president agreed to the use of the new weapon. Groves mentioned that he believed Truman's decision "was one of noninterference – basically a decision not to upset the existing plan." The committee also recommended that an atomic bomb be used as soon as possible, without warning to maximize shock and against a "war plant ... surrounded by workers' houses." The last point may have been added to increase any psychological impact on the Japanese people, despite signaling the destruction of an entire city and its inhabitants. Before Truman left for the 17 July–2 August 1945 Potsdam conference, the committee also suggested telling the Soviet leader Josef Stalin about America's new nuclear capability, Truman agreed. Security concerns about leaking nuclear secrets to the Soviets were widespread, but Truman would circumvent these by telling Stalin about the atomic bomb.

Field Marshal Hata Shunroku was responsible for the defense of Kyushu. As commander of the Second General Army Headquarters, he ordered the construction of extensive defensive works throughout the island. He survived the atomic bombing of Hiroshima where his headquarters was stationed. (US Army)

A DEMONSTRATION OF POWER

On the day before the opening of the Potsdam conference, Groves and the Manhattan Project personnel conducted an operational test on their experimental plutonium bomb at Trinity, New Mexico. The "gadget" detonated perfectly, resulting in four times the expected explosive power at 18.6 kilotons. The test result moved Oppenheimer and his colleagues to realize the impact of their work; at the same time, some began to doubt the use of their talents to make such a terrible and devastating weapon. Truman learned about the test on 17 July, with more details reaching him on 21 July. The president discussed the test with Churchill, and notified Stalin. Churchill

had already given his prior approval to use the bomb in accordance with a previous agreement with the late president Roosevelt.

There is some disagreement about when and how the decision was made to use the atomic bomb. At Potsdam, Truman did authorize General Carl Spaatz, the new commander of Strategic Air Forces in the Pacific, to prepare to drop the bombs not earlier than 3 August, based on a 25 July memorandum, provided that the weather conditions were right for this. Spaatz had insisted on a written order for this operation. In the directive, Truman retained the absolute right to use the bomb or not.

On 26 July, the United States, Britain and China released a declaration calling for Japan's immediate surrender. It also called for the dismemberment of the nation's remaining empire, demobilization of all military forces, trials for war criminals and the elimination of Japan's capacity to act in a belligerent fashion in the future. It did not ease the requirements for unconditional surrender, but remained ambiguous about how the Japanese people might determine the form of their future government; the declaration did not declare a direct end or continuation of the imperial dynasty. Some Truman administration officials thought that Tokyo might view this condition as allowing the possibility of retaining the emperor. The members of Prime Minister Suzuki Kantaro's government had argued about accepting a peace offer. Military members of the cabinet wanted to continue the war. On 29 July Suzuki, for domestic political reasons, expressed to the Japanese press his impression that the Potsdam Declaration was nothing new and held no "significant value." Truman and his administration regarded this as a rejection of the declaration. The readying of the atomic bombs went ahead. Truman gave the final approval to drop the atomic bomb on 2 August, on his way home from Potsdam.

Late in the war, B-29s and other aircraft could attack Japanese targets almost without opposition. This B-29 flying over Mount Fuji symbolizes the air superiority of the Allies over Japan. (US Air Force)

509TH COMPOSITE GROUP

The War Department activated the 509th Composite Group on 17 December 1944 as part of the Second Air Force's 315th Bombardment Wing, under the command of Colonel Paul Tibbets. It contained the 393rd Bombardment Squadron (Very Heavy) plus technical support squadrons. Tibbets was made aware of the Manhattan Project in September 1944 and was told to prepare a B-29 unit to drop nuclear weapons. The organization of the 509th CG was unique among other composite groups, being totally self-supporting. Arnold gave Tibbets a wide latitude of authority and almost unlimited access to resources by use of a special codeword, Silverplate, which indicated the USAAF's highest priority.

Tibbets established his training facility at Wendover Field, Utah on the Nevada state border. This remote and desolate location allowed the hand-picked B-29 crews to hone their navigation and bombing skills. Officials maintained strict security measures regarding all activities on the base. Tibbets' crews practiced long-distance bombing runs from Wendover to the Salton Sea in southern California. Visual bombing was deemed the preferred method of delivery for the bomb, despite the winds at high altitude; concerns about inaccurate B-29 radar guidance persuaded Tibbets to opt for visual bombing. Radar guidance accuracy was relatively poor in 1945: for example, a B-29 crew had only a one to two percent chance of dropping a bomb in a target circle of 1,000ft radius. In clear weather, a visual bomb release increased the chance of success to between 20 and 50 percent. Tibbets' crews consistently hit targets within a 300ft-radius circle. The 10 B-29s of the 509th CG also trained in Batista, Cuba from 15 to 31 January. The crews tested their abilities to fly long navigational missions over water and to conduct high-altitude visual and radar bombing, in the course of 42 flying training hours.

Before Tibbet's 509th CG could drop any nuclear weapon, the crews would need an appropriate Pacific base. Fortunately, Nimitz's advance had taken most of the Mariana Islands by July 1944. While Tibbets finished training in Cuba, King sent Commander Frederic L. Ashworth, assigned to the Manhattan Project to support fusing and detonation testing, to explain the atomic bomb and clear the way for a 509th CG base. Tinian, an island 12 miles long and about 38 square miles in size, was selected. The island thus became one massive airfield. The 509th CG operations would be located on the island's North Field. Navy Seabees (construction and civil engineers) had to build special laboratories and storage facilities for the atomic bombs and the group. 509th CG ground echelon personnel started to leave Wendover for Tinian on 26 April 1945. The unit's B-29s began to arrive in June.

Tibbet's 509th CG was transferred to the Twentieth Air Force for administrative purposes and placed under the XXI Bomber Command and General Curtis LeMay. The atomic bomb mission had a convoluted command structure. The Joint Chiefs of Staff were largely left out of the chain of command. LeMay was Tibbet's nominal commander; however, Groves still had extensive control over the operation through his deputy Brigadier General Thomas Farrell on Tinian. The XXI Bomber Command would determine when the atomic bomb mission was launched, based on suitable weather conditions. Even at this stage, General of the Air Force Henry "Hap" Arnold and LeMay were still skeptical about the Manhattan Project; they thought B-29 incendiary and high-explosive bombing operations would suffice to end the war soon. LeMay even questioned the 509th CG pilots'

Marquis Kido Koichi, Lord Keeper of the Privy Seal, was a personal adviser to Emperor Hirohito. Kido sided with parties who wanted to end the war. He was influential in getting Hirohito to accept the Allies' unconditional surrender terms. (US Army)

Foreign Minister Togo Shigenori pressed Prime Minister Suzuki and Emperor Hirohito to accept surrender. Togo clashed with IJA and IJN officials over the issue of continuing the war and trying to negotiate surrender by making a final battle costly to American forces. This photograph was taken during his incarceration before his 1946 trial for war crimes. (US Army)

General Umezu Yoshijiro, Chief of the Army General Staff, expressed severe doubts that the Japanese military would accept any surrender. IJA and IJN members were ingrained with the idea that it was a military crime to surrender, and that one should die fighting. (US Army)

ability to conduct the mission; he wanted seasoned Pacific B-29 veteran crews to drop the nuclear cargo. Lieutenant General Nathan F. Twining replaced LeMay as commander of the XXI Bomber Command on 1 August. Twining would ultimately issue the direct field orders to Tibbets to drop the atomic bomb. However, LeMay remained as Carl Spaatz's chief of staff with authority to launch Tibbets' aircraft.

While the IJA and IJN prepared for an invasion, the USAAF continued to bomb Japan. The 509th CG crews needed to orient themselves to the navigational challenges, weather, long distances and geography, and become acclimatized to combat conditions. The crews started training at Tinian on 30 June, and conventional operational missions over Japan began on 20 July. The crews trained using "pumpkins" – specially constructed bombs that simulated the nuclear weapons in color and shape – to practice handling and releasing an atomic bomb. Crews also practiced appropriate navigational procedures, visual bomb release, dropping the weapon at about 30,000ft and conducting a high-speed, radical turn to avoid the nuclear effects after bomb detonation. On the first mission, one 509th CG B-29 sought an alternate target in Tokyo. The crew attempted to drop their 10,000 lb "pumpkin" on the Imperial Palace, but missed. Had the crew been successful and killed the emperor, it might have affected the decision-making process in Japan; the Japanese people's willingness to continue the war might have been strengthened by the emperor's death, with military leaders seizing control of the country and ordering their units to continue fighting. XXI Bomber Command units avoided targeting Hiroshima, Niigata, Kokura and Nagasaki during these runs. In total, Tibbets sent his crews on numerous combat missions that involved attacks on 28 cities and the dropping of 49 "pumpkins." The 509th CG lost no aircraft conducting these missions.

READYING THE WEAPONS

While Tibbets perfected the method of delivery, Manhattan Project scientists and engineers started to prepare the Little Boy and Fat Man weapons for operational use. War and Navy Department officials gave the highest priority for transportation and security for the nuclear components and assemblies. The 509th CG's 1st Ordnance Squadron and the 1st Technical Services Detachment, War Department (composed of Navy, security, scientists and other technical specialists) would assemble the two nuclear devices on Tinian. Physicians and psychologists would also assess the impact of the nuclear detonation on the Japanese. Some weapon assemblies were delivered by C-54 and B-29 aircraft from Kirtland Field near Albuquerque, New Mexico to Tinian. The cruiser USS *Indianapolis* had delivered the Little Boy fissionable material to Tinian from San Francisco on 26 July. On 30 July, the Japanese submarine *I-58* attacked the *Indianapolis* with six torpedoes while the American ship was en route to Guam. The *Indianapolis*, which was traveling without any escort ships at night, took two hits and sank. Out of a crew of 1,196 officers and men, the US Navy would rescue only 316 survivors, who spent four days in the water. Unfortunately, no radio message was sent to air-sea rescue.

HIROSHIMA

Tibbets awaited field orders from XXI Bomber Command headquarters allowing him to drop the first atomic bomb. He had asked for LeMay's recommendation on the primary target, and both agreed that Hiroshima had a major military presence and seemed the most valuable selection. Hiroshima thus became the primary target, but depending on the weather conditions, the B-29 carrying Little Boy could divert to two alternative targets. USAAF, Navy and civilian specialists labored with Little Boy's assembly and completed most of the bomb's construction by 31 July. All that was needed to make it an operational weapon was the insertion of cordite charges to fire the uranium "bullet" through the gun device to the uranium core. For safety reasons, a detonation expert would emplace the charges into Little Boy after aircraft take-off: this would reduce the risk of a nuclear explosion if the B-29 crashed. B-29 take-off accidents were frequent occurrences because of engine problems and other malfunctions. The crew carrying the atomic bomb also had to be careful descending once Little Boy was armed; the primary radar or a back-up barometric fuse might cause the weapon to explode if the plane descended too rapidly with the fuses in place.

Major Thomas V. Ferebee was the 509th CG's best bombardier. He released Little Boy over Hiroshima. (US Air Force)

The 16 July 1945 Trinity, New Mexico test of a plutonium device demonstrated the great power of the atomic bomb. Truman was impressed, but others were not sure that it should be used. (Department of Energy)

If the B-29 were forced to return to the Marianas or to make an emergency landing at Iwo Jima or Okinawa, then the charges were to be removed and the atomic bomb returned to Tinian. Iwo Jima was important for another reason. Its former Japanese air defense units had given Tokyo at least two hours' warning of any B-29s heading to Japan. The capture of Iwo Jima reduced the chances of the Japanese intercepting any B-29s, especially those from the 509th CG. B-29 crews would arrive at Tinian with the Fat Man assemblies on 2 August. There was no more fissionable material available to build another bomb at that point.

The 509th CG was ready to deliver Little Boy on 1 August, well ahead of Truman's directive to initiate operations by 3 August. Only adverse weather conditions could delay the launch. Brigadier General Thomas Farrell was prepared to stop operations if directed by Groves, after Truman had given approval to use the atomic bomb on 2 August. Tibbets and LeMay's decision about Hiroshima was forwarded to XXI Bomber Command. Lieutenant General Nathan Twining, commander of XXI Bomber Command, approved the coordinated decision on Hiroshima under 509th CG Field Order No. 13 on 2 August. All seemed ready for the bombing. The only missing piece was the revelation of the 509th CG's true purpose to the B-29 crews who would execute the mission.

Tibbets and others briefed the crews on 4 August about the mission. Initially, only Tibbets had known details about the Manhattan Project and the unit's connection to this secretive organization. By 1 August, Lieutenant Colonel Hazen J. Payette, group intelligence officer, and Captain Joseph Bucher, another intelligence officer, were informed of the 509th CG's mission. Tibbets, however, would not disclose that the weapon contained a nuclear device, just that the bomb would be "powerful" and could "end the war"; scientists estimated the bomb had a yield of up to 20,000 tons (20 kilotons) of TNT. The release of information about the nature of the atomic bomb would be made public by Truman after the "gadget" had been dropped. For his part, Nimitz had been briefed in February by Commander Frederic Ashworth of the Manhattan Project, while MacArthur learned about the mission only in July. Tibbets also told Major Charles V. Sweeney, commander of the 393rd Bombardment Squadron, and Tibbets' deputy and former 393rd commander, Lieutenant Colonel Thomas J. Clausen. The aircrews were given

The path of the *Enola Gay* to Hiroshima and the route of the USS *Indianapolis*

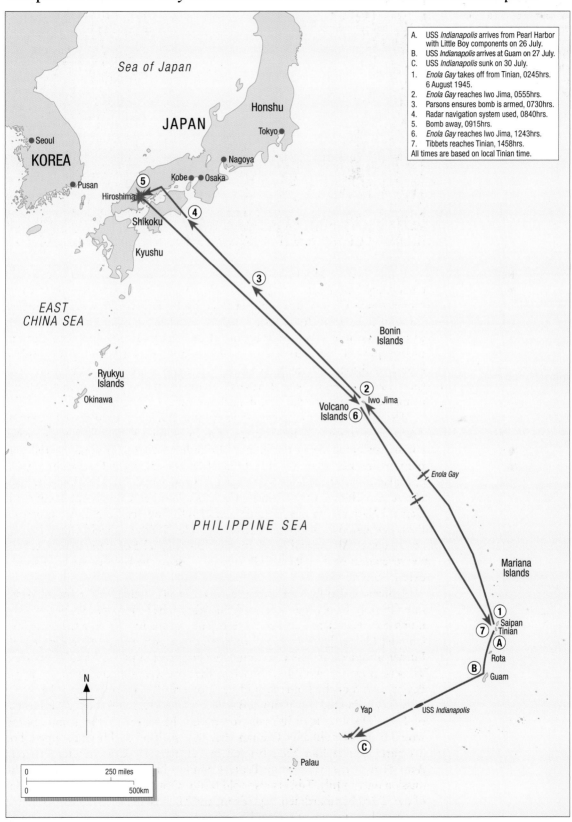

A. USS *Indianapolis* arrives from Pearl Harbor with Little Boy components on 26 July.
B. USS *Indianapolis* arrives at Guam on 27 July.
C. USS *Indianapolis* sunk on 30 July.
1. *Enola Gay* takes off from Tinian, 0245hrs. 6 August 1945.
2. *Enola Gay* reaches Iwo Jima, 0555hrs.
3. Parsons ensures bomb is armed, 0730hrs.
4. Radar navigation system used, 0840hrs.
5. Bomb away, 0915hrs.
6. *Enola Gay* reaches Iwo Jima, 1243hrs.
7. Tibbets reaches Tinian, 1458hrs.
All times are based on local Tinian time.

ABOVE, LEFT
The USS *Indianapolis* carried key Little Boy components to Tinian. After they had been delivered, the ship was sunk by a Japanese submarine with great loss of life. (US Navy)

ABOVE, RIGHT
The *Enola Gay* crew just before take-off. Parsons and Jeppson were checking Little Boy and so missed this photograph. (US Air Force)

information about the targets, bomb-dropping procedures and the likely effects of the explosion. Subsequent briefings included air-sea rescue procedures and weather data.

THE PLAN OF ATTACK

Hiroshima is located on the southern half of Honshu. The city faces the western side of Shikoku with an open port to the Inland Sea, the body of water separating Honshu, Shikoku and Kyushu. Hiroshima was the largest city untouched by the Twentieth Air Force B-29 raids. The city offered a very tempting target since the topography of the area could focus and concentrate Little Boy's effect. Typical B-29 incendiary attacks relied on spreading fires to destroy the target; the urban area around Hiroshima was separated by several waterways, a part of the Ota River delta. This geographic situation did not lend itself to a firebombing raid; Little Boy might have more success. The city's population had fallen from a prewar total of about 400,000 to less than 300,000. The IJA had also stationed about 43,000 troops in the area and it would have been a major staging area. Japanese industry still operated military production plants in the vicinity, but evacuation from the city had reduced its labor force. The city turned out heavy weapons, aircraft parts, precision tools, machinery, chemicals, steel and foodstuffs. Increased emphasis on *Ketsu-Go*, loss of male labor for military service, evacuation and other disruptions forced Japanese industry to use more women and children as labor to support military production. To make matters worse, the US blockade had reduced the flow of raw materials from other areas, preventing production from remaining at peak levels.

Tibbets had decided that he would pilot the aircraft carrying the atomic bomb to Hiroshima. He would also send three weather reconnaissance aircraft to Hiroshima, Kokura and Nagasaki; Niigata was excluded from the mission probably owing to concerns about the weather. These aircraft crews would report weather conditions, which in turn would be used to determine whether a B-29 could drop Little Boy by visual means. By using three weather reconnaissance aircraft, Tibbets would receive the most accurate target information possible. Communist Chinese guerillas supplied details of the conditions over northern China, which meteorologists used to forecast Japanese weather conditions. With up-to-date weather information, Tibbets, while in flight, would decide which target he would attack. There could be at most only 30 percent cloud cover and light winds over any selected target. One major problem for the aircraft crews was caused by the treacherous jet stream crosswinds present at high altitudes: these winds, which could reach up to 200 miles per hour, could shift aircraft off course and affect bombing accuracy.

Tibbet's B-29 would carry Little Boy, while another would provide photographic and observation support so that Manhattan Project and USAAF analysts could compare pre- and post-strike conditions. The XXI Bomber Command had also scheduled two unarmed F-13 aircraft (modified camera-carrying B-29s) from the 3rd Photographic Reconnaissance Squadron to provide post-strike imagery a few hours after the Little Boy detonation. A sixth aircraft carried scientific instruments to measure the impact of the explosion of the atomic bomb. This aircraft employed special radio receivers that would gather data from three parachute-equipped devices that transmitted measurements back to the aircraft over the impact area. The last assigned aircraft was stationed at Iwo Jima. If the original Tinian bomber was unable to continue its mission, then a ground crew would remove Little Boy and put it in the standby B-29 to continue the mission. If no target were available because of poor weather, a crew member would disarm Little Boy in flight and the aircraft would be flown to Iwo Jima for bomb removal.

Adverse weather pushed back the mission start date. LeMay, Spaatz's chief of staff, was responsible for determining when weather conditions would allow Tibbets to drop Little Boy. The extra time allowed for additional crew preparation. The aircraft that would follow Tibbets into the target area would have to make a high-speed 155-degree turn to avoid the biggest concern – the explosive shockwave. Additionally, the B-29s had to ensure there was a distance of at least eight miles between themselves and the impact point. Some concern was raised about enemy air defenses, given that there were to be only three B-29s in the immediate operational area: IJAAF and IJNAF interceptors and antiaircraft artillery might concentrate against these few US aircraft. Fortunately for the American air crews, the bomb release, even in daylight,

Little Boy was the codename for the uranium 235-armed bomb that would be dropped on Hiroshima. Its detonation would be the second manmade nuclear explosion in history. (National Archives)

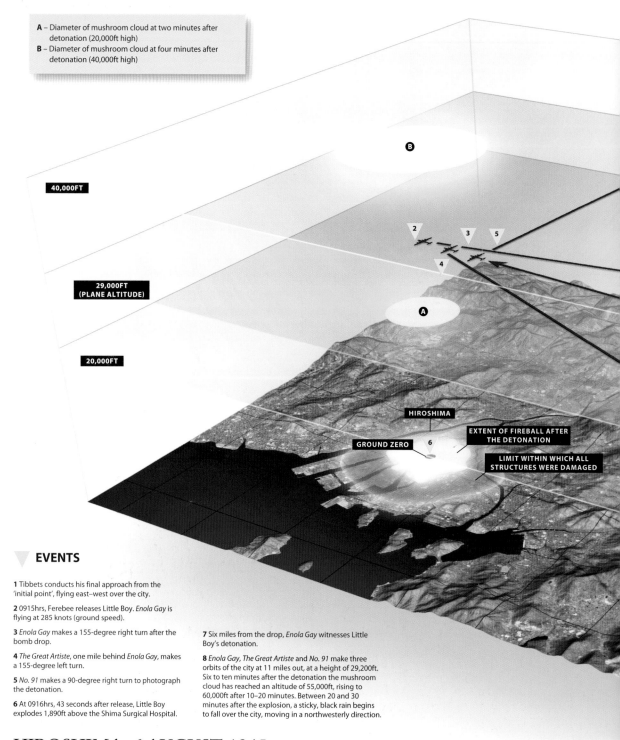

A – Diameter of mushroom cloud at two minutes after detonation (20,000ft high)
B – Diameter of mushroom cloud at four minutes after detonation (40,000ft high)

B

40,000FT

29,000FT
(PLANE ALTITUDE)

A

20,000FT

HIROSHIMA

GROUND ZERO

EXTENT OF FIREBALL AFTER THE DETONATION

LIMIT WITHIN WHICH ALL STRUCTURES WERE DAMAGED

EVENTS

1 Tibbets conducts his final approach from the 'initial point', flying east–west over the city.

2 0915hrs, Ferebee releases Little Boy. *Enola Gay* is flying at 285 knots (ground speed).

3 *Enola Gay* makes a 155-degree right turn after the bomb drop.

4 *The Great Artiste*, one mile behind *Enola Gay*, makes a 155-degree left turn.

5 *No. 91* makes a 90-degree right turn to photograph the detonation.

6 At 0916hrs, 43 seconds after release, Little Boy explodes 1,890ft above the Shima Surgical Hospital.

7 Six miles from the drop, *Enola Gay* witnesses Little Boy's detonation.

8 *Enola Gay, The Great Artiste* and *No. 91* make three orbits of the city at 11 miles out, at a height of 29,200ft. Six to ten minutes after the detonation the mushroom cloud has reached an altitude of 55,000ft, rising to 60,000ft after 10–20 minutes. Between 20 and 30 minutes after the explosion, a sticky, black rain begins to fall over the city, moving in a northwesterly direction.

HIROSHIMA, 6 AUGUST 1945

The routes of *Enola Gay*, *The Great Artiste* and *Aircraft No. 91* (later named *Necessary Evil*) during the mission to drop Little Boy over Hiroshima. On 6 August, there was less than 30 percent cloud cover over Hiroshima. *Enola Gay* flew from east to west over the city, and at 0915 hrs, Ferebee released Little Boy. The uranium device detonated some 43 seconds after it was dropped.

Note: gridlines are shown at intervals of 2 miles/3.2km

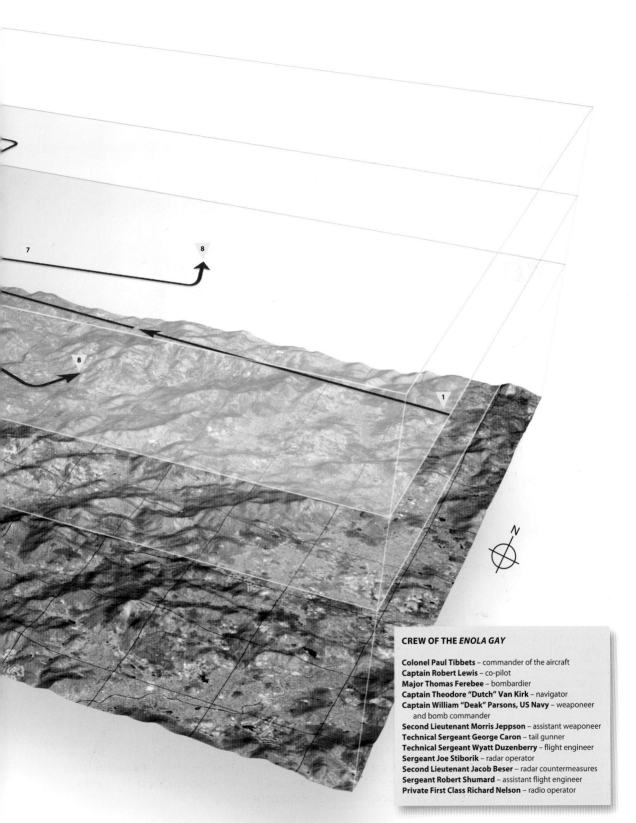

7

8

8

1

N

CREW OF THE *ENOLA GAY*

Colonel Paul Tibbets – commander of the aircraft
Captain Robert Lewis – co-pilot
Major Thomas Ferebee – bombardier
Captain Theodore "Dutch" Van Kirk – navigator
Captain William "Deak" Parsons, US Navy – weaponeer
 and bomb commander
Second Lieutenant Morris Jeppson – assistant weaponeer
Technical Sergeant George Caron – tail gunner
Technical Sergeant Wyatt Duzenberry – flight engineer
Sergeant Joe Stiborik – radar operator
Second Lieutenant Jacob Beser – radar countermeasures
Sergeant Robert Shumard – assistant flight engineer
Private First Class Richard Nelson – radio operator

57

would take place above the range of heavy antiaircraft artillery fire, and the weakened state of the IJAAF and the IJNAF suggested that a massed interception would not occur against a high-altitude attack.

The 509th CG Silverplate B-29s did not have gun turrets, save for those for the tail guns, in order to reduce weight and increase bomb-load capacity and speed. This was not an unusual practice in the Pacific. B-29 speed and the ability to fly at high altitudes could help avoid relatively slow-reacting interceptors and B-29s often did not use their guns. The single weather reconnaissance B-29 that would check cloud coverage over the target would probably not elicit a significant Japanese reaction anyway. Engineers and scientists had also estimated that the optimal altitude from which to drop the nuclear weapon was (for safety reasons) between 28,000 and 30,000ft. This would create a buffer allowing the aircraft to escape the expected shockwave and blast effects. Once released, Little Boy's timing device would arm the atomic bomb at 5,000ft, with detonation set for 1,850ft altitude. A radar detection system built into the bomb's four fins would determine the height of the bomb and activate the gun device that would initiate the nuclear explosion. Detonation at too low an altitude would force the blast, heat and shock effects into the ground – too high an altitude and the three effects would be dissipated into the atmosphere. Little or nothing was known about the effects of radiation: nuclear science was still in its infancy.

RED PLUGS FOR GO

The 509th CG tested the sequence for arming and dropping Little Boy on 5 August. That day crews dropped practice weapons successfully and the 509th completed almost all the steps in the lead-up to the mission against Japan. USAAF meteorologists believed weather conditions had improved sufficiently over western Japan to allow visual bombing. As a result, LeMay approved the first atomic bombing mission at 1400hrs on 5 August, to take place the next day. Once LeMay released the 509th CG, Operations Order No. 35 was issued throughout the group to initiate immediate action. This order provided specific timetables and actions for the unit. USAAF and USN officials had ironed out the remaining details such as air-sea rescue procedures for any downed crews, which would be executed by specially equipped USAAF and USN aircraft and submarines. Restrictions on USAAF or USN aircraft from entering the target areas four hours before and six hours after the attack would prevent them from interfering with the operation. Twining ensured diversionary attacks by 604 B-29s throughout Japan would also take place on 6 August.

The three weather reconnaissance B-29 aircraft preceded Tibbets' and the other two support aircraft that would now conduct "Special Bombing Mission No. 13" as it was known. *Jabbitt III*, piloted by Major John Wilson, would survey Kokura. Major Ralph Taylor, in *Full House*, was responsible for reporting on Nagasaki. Captain Claude Eatherly, who had conducted the 20 July attack on the Imperial Palace, would fly in *Straight Flush* to reconnoiter Hiroshima. Sweeney, flying in *The Great Artiste*, carried a scientific instrument package and would follow Tibbets in the bomb run. The photographic mission fell to Major George W. Marquardt's B-29, in *Aircraft No. 91*. Standing by at Iwo Jima was Captain Charles McKnight and his B-29, *Top Secret*. Tibbets would fly B-29 *No. 82*; at the time the aircraft was unnamed, although Tibbets would later christen her *Enola Gay* after his mother.

This rear shot of the *Enola Gay* shows Little Boy in the bomb loading pit. The mission went off almost perfectly. (US Air Force)

Other USAAF crews stationed at Tinian were curious about the arrival of and secrecy surrounding the 509th CG. Only one bombardment squadron in an unusual "composite" group seemed odd, since most bombardment groups had four combat squadrons. The inordinate amount of support and priority in terms of resources and facilities produced questions and cynical calls that the 509th CG was winning the war all by itself, a prophetic taunt that would soon have a ring of truth about it. The 509th CG's tail insignia, a horizontal arrowhead enclosed in a circle, was replaced by a different bombardment group insignia. The *Enola Gay* would sport an encircled "R" that denoted the 6th Bombardment Group from the 313th Bombardment Wing, to confuse any Japanese intelligence effort to discover the unit's identity or the reason for its presence in the Pacific.

Tibbets also selected the key crew members for the flight. Major Thomas V. Ferebee, the group's staff bombardier and Captain Theodore J. "Dutch" Van Kirk, the 509th CG's staff navigator, would perform those functions. These two experts were the best in the group. USN Captain William "Deak" Parsons, a member of the Manhattan Project, also went along. He had headed the effort to develop a system to detonate the atomic bomb. Parsons took along an electronics officer, Second Lieutenant Morris Jeppson, as an assistant, who would monitor Little Boy and any efforts by the enemy to use electronic jamming which might affect the bomb's delivery.

Briefings continued all night from 5 August into the early morning hours of 6 August. The weather aircraft began their missions at 0137hrs (all times cited are based on local Tinian time, Hiroshima time being an hour earlier). McKnight soon followed at 0151hrs for his duties at Iwo Jima. *Enola Gay* and her two escorts would take off about an hour later. Tibbets left Tinian at 0245hrs. The *Enola Gay*, *The Great Artiste* and Marquardt's plane would take about three hours to rendezvous over Iwo Jima. Groves insisted that photographers record the activities for posterity. William Laurence, a reporter for *The New York Times* was allowed to take part in the mission, and also to report on the events. He would go on to win the Pulitzer Prize for his work.

After Tibbets had taken off and was heading towards Iwo Jima, Parsons and Jeppson armed Little Boy. Parsons inserted the cordite plugs and a detonator. Jeppson was responsible for ensuring that three green safety plugs

THE AGE OF NUCLEAR WAR IS BORN (pp. 60–61)

The *Enola Gay* (1) delivered the world's first operational atomic weapon on Hiroshima. The 6 August attack came as a complete surprise to the Japanese government. USAAF aircraft had already pummeled most large and medium-sized Japanese cities by means of high altitude, precision daylight and low-altitude incendiary night raids on targets. The Hiroshima mission was an attempt to shock Tokyo into acceptance of unconditional surrender terms reiterated by the Potsdam Declaration. Little Boy, a uranium bomb, detonated within a minute of being released from the *Enola Gay*.

Following Little Boy's detonation, a blinding flash occured. Intense heat and blast effects soon developed. Tibbets had turned the aircraft and was six miles away from ground zero at the time of the explosion. From his tail gunner position, George Caron witnessed the result. He described seeing "a shockwave of compressed air that was shaped like a ring around a planet." Caron vividly recalled that looking into the growing mushroom cloud (2) was like a "peep into hell."

Approximately 30 seconds after the bomb's explosion, a devastating firestorm was created, which turned into a tornado. Later, a heavy "black rain" of debris and radioactive material fell on the northwest part of Hiroshima. The heaviest rain lasted for about an hour. Where rain fell into rivers and streams, eye witnesses reported that all the fish in them died. Other reports noted that when cattle ate the grass where the rain had fallen, they too fell sick and died.

Following notification from Parsons of the massive destruction caused, Groves reported the damage to Marshall and Stimson. President Truman would announce to the world the first operational use of the atomic bomb the following day.

were inserted into the weapon to inhibit stray electrical current that would prematurely detonate the bomb.

At 0555hrs, the *Enola Gay* reached Iwo Jima. The crew circled over the island until the two escort aircraft caught up with them. Since leaving Tinian, the B-29s had started a slow ascent that would bring the aircraft to over 30,000ft altitude. Tibbets was pushing the aircraft at an indicated air speed of about 200 knots; the aircrews did not experience any severe winds, and so the aircraft continued without any problems until they reached Japan. The *Enola Gay* was heading towards the Japanese home islands ready to strike. At 0730hrs Jeppson replaced the green safety plugs with red ones to arm the bomb, and Parsons informed Tibbets that the first atomic bomb was now operational. Little Boy was armed and ready.

The weather aircraft were the key to determining where Tibbets and the other aircraft would head for. All three weather reports indicated that the targets were relatively clear. Eatherly's report to Tibbets indicated that Hiroshima had less than 30 percent cloud cover. The weather at about 15,000ft comprised scattered clouds at about 20 percent cover, with similar conditions at lower altitudes. Tibbets received the weather report at 0815hrs. *Straight Flush*'s presence had alerted the Japanese defenders to an enemy presence and a warning was made to Hiroshima civilians to take cover at 0809hrs. No enemy interceptors could reach the B-29, flying at 30,200ft, to shoot it down, and the alert was canceled at 0831 hrs. Eatherly's report ensured that Hiroshima became the focus of the *Enola Gay*'s mission. The other two weather reconnaissance missions reported after *Straight Flush*, but Tibbets had already decided to drop Little Boy on Hiroshima.

The aircraft had flown over Shikoku, then had crossed over Honshu west to Hiroshima. While on the approach to the target, Van Kirk noted in his navigator's log that seven ships where in harbor at Omi-shima (he identified the location as "Mishima"), which was southeast of Hiroshima. The *Enola Gay now* needed to pick up speed and gain altitude.

Tibbets was on his final approach, which required the *Enola Gay* to fly from east to west over the city. As planned, Tibbets used an intersection of two of Hiroshima's rivers, the Ota and Motoyasu, as the aiming point for the 10ft-long atomic weapon. Little Boy's 8,900 lb weight would explode about two miles from Hiroshima Castle above the T-shaped Aioi Bridge. The bomb would detonate over the center of the city. At 0912hrs, Tibbets passed the initial point and was at a recorded altitude of 31,060ft (as detailed in Van Kirk's logbook; some accounts indicate the altitude was 31,600ft). Cloud cover over the city was now about 10 percent. The Japanese Chugokyu District Army Information Center had sounded an air raid warning at 0913 hrs after reports had arrived of three B-29s over the Saijo area. The warning was too late to allow any interceptors to become airborne, and the *Enola Gay* was flying too high for antiaircraft artillery to reach her. At about 0915hrs, Ferebee released Little Boy; the aircraft was flying over 285 knots ground speed, and immediately began its turn away to escape the imminent explosion. The crews of the three B-29s donned Polaroid goggles to protect themselves from the blinding flash to was to follow detonation.

Little Boy hurtled down towards the Aioi Bridge. After dropping five miles, the fin radar system activated the detonator. At 0916hrs, some 43 seconds after it was dropped from *Enola Gay*'s bomb bay, the weapon exploded at 1,890ft above the ground. Tibbets and the crew were about six miles away after turning sharply away from their previous position above the Aioi Bridge. Ferebee's aim,

Tibbets' crew dropped Little Boy on Hiroshima at 0915hrs, with detonation following under a minute later. This photograph was taken at 0918hrs. (US Air Force)

however, was off; he missed the bridge by about 800ft and Little Boy detonated over the Shima Surgical Hospital. Scientists estimated that Little Boy's actual bomb yield was about 15,000 tons of TNT. One postwar analysis indicated that it would have required 210 B-29s with a combination of incendiary and high explosive ordnance to have done the same job.

Tibbets finally announced that the crew had dropped the first atomic bomb in history. He reported results as "excellent." The brilliance of the explosion was "10 times that of the sun," according to witnesses over five miles away, and the B-29 aircrews encountered two shock waves. Hiroshima residents would call the bomb *Pika-don* or "flashboom." On the ground, the immediate area around the center of the blast was heated to 1 million degrees Celsius; the maximum temperature reached was 50 million degrees at the core. People, animals, buildings and other items were immediately incinerated or vaporized in the central area beneath the explosion. In the wider area, the blast effects crushed unreinforced buildings before setting fire to them. The casualty toll was horrific. Hiroshima police officials estimated that immediate casualties comprised 71,379 killed or missing. The bomb caused over 68,023 wounded (19,691 seriously). After the war, the March 1947 United States Strategic Bombing Survey (USSBS) estimated Little Boy killed 60,000 to 80,000 people. A 10 August 1946 estimate pushed deaths from the raid up to 118,661 and missing persons at 3,677. Later, perhaps with the inclusion of the effects of radiation sickness or more accurate accounting, Japanese officials recorded 30,524 seriously wounded and 48,606 slightly wounded.

A growing mushroom cloud of highly radioactive dust and debris grew to a height of 20,000ft two minutes after detonation. After eight minutes, USAAF crews could see the mushroom cloud from 390 miles away. The dust cloud pushed up to about 60,000ft, its maximum height. Later a thick, black, radioactive rain fell on the area below the cloud.

The USAAF F-13s had difficulty producing post-strike reconnaissance data owing to the lack of visibility over the target area in the immediate aftermath of the attack. Smoke, fire and dust covered the city. Only after 11 August did the XXI Bomber Command intelligence analysts release a bomb damage assessment report, having gathered aerial photographs. The city's center was devastated; just over four square miles out of an urban center of seven square miles were flattened – about 60 percent of the city's area. A further 0.6 square miles were damaged. More than 75 percent of the city's 90,000 buildings were destroyed. Fire overwhelmed the city and contributed to many deaths and injuries. Unfortunately, Hiroshima did contain some USAAF prisoners of war, who were killed in the explosion. The photographic analysts estimated that an IJA division headquarters was completely destroyed, the Army Food Depot was 25 percent damaged and other targets received some damage. Surprisingly, the city could still provide some services to her population almost immediately after the attack.

Meanwhile, the B-29s involved in the mission returned safely to Tinian. Once the *Enola Gay* had landed, Spaatz awarded the Distinguished Service Cross to Tibbets and Distinguished Flying Crosses to the rest of the crew.

Truman was notified of the raid while returning from Potsdam aboard the cruiser USS *Augusta*. He enthusiastically declared: "This is the greatest thing in history." He released a pre-approved statement that described the bomb, and further warned that if Japan did not accept the Potsdam Declaration "they may expect a rain of ruin from the air, the like of which has never been seen on this earth." Truman had only the plutonium Fat Man device left to use, but he had been informed that a third bomb might be ready sometime in August. Some American military leaders, such as Spaatz, LeMay, Twining and Nimitz, believed this third nuclear device should be dropped on Tokyo if no surrender was forthcoming. As more information was received, it became clear that the earliest the 509th CG could drop this third weapon would be 22 August.

The initial reaction to Hiroshima from the Japanese government was mixed. The IJA and IJN military leadership received fragmentary reports on what had taken place there throughout 6 August, as communications with Hiroshima had been cut. Personnel at the naval base at Kure, south of Hiroshima, witnessed the detonation and had contacted IJN Headquarters. American and British radio broadcasts notified ordinary Japanese civilians and their government of the atomic bomb attack early on 7 August. The next day, Tokyo issued a press release confirming that Hiroshima had been bombed, but did not indicate that the United States had dropped an atomic weapon.

The Japanese military had previously attempted to build an atomic bomb, but the lack of uranium and other resources, and of technical personnel in particular, precluded any significant progress. Some IJA officers and scientists believed that the attack had not been accomplished by a nuclear weapon, since they themselves had been unable to build one. They speculated that Hiroshima was a victim of a larger conventional weapon, and in the light of this were remained determined to continue the war. Conversely, some members of the Japanese cabinet feared that the United States now possessed a weapon that could destroy the entire nation: for them, peace was the only

Paul Tibbets and the crew of *Enola Gay* returned to Tinian in triumph. From Tibbets' perspective, almost everything about the 6 August 1945 mission was a success. (US Air Force)

Tibbets was awarded the Distinguished Service Cross by General Carl Spaatz after the Hiroshima mission. Tibbets would retire as a brigadier general in August 1966. (US Air Force)

option. A few Japanese senior officials accurately speculated that even if America had used an atomic bomb, they would not have many more. At a 7 August cabinet meeting, Foreign Minister Togo Shigenori, an advocate of negotiating with the United States, used this opportunity to suggest that Tokyo accept the Potsdam Declaration. Prime Minister Suzuki, a veteran Japanese government official, suggested to Togo that he inform Hirohito of Hiroshima's destruction and that reports seemed to indicate that it was caused by an atomic bomb. Hirohito had actually already been informed of the Hiroshima bombing and was "overwhelmed with grief." He indicated that the war must be ended.

IJA and IJN technical teams began to arrive in Hiroshima on 8 August to examine what had happened, and were reportedly overcome by the destruction they witnessed before them. Their conclusion was that the B-29s had used an atomic bomb on 6 August. Hata, the Second General Army commander, whose headquarters was in Hiroshima and who was responsible for defenses on Kyushu, indicated that the atomic bomb had not been as deadly as first thought. Although the Hiroshima Castle and his headquarters had been obliterated, he continued to show a resilient desire to fight.

Togo met with the emperor on August 8 and warned Hirohito that the atomic bomb was a massive threat and that the Americans would incinerate the rest of Japan with a storm of atomic devices. If the Potsdam Declaration was not accepted by Tokyo, more attacks might follow. Hirohito told Togo to inform Suzuki, who was responsible for gaining unanimity among the cabinet, to start surrender procedures. Meanwhile, to increase pressure on the Japanese, the USAAF used more conventional B-29 raids. A total of 412 B-29s struck the Nakajima aircraft plant in a daylight attack on Musashino on 8 August. Six 509th CG B-29s dropped five "pumpkins" that day to maintain a state of operational readiness for any future missions.

NAGASAKI

In the wake of the destruction of Hiroshima, Washington had to convince the Japanese government and people that Little Boy was not an isolated experimental device, and that the unconditional surrender demand remained as strong as ever. The Soviet Union's declaration of war against Japan and Moscow's invasion into Japanese-held territories might still force capitulation without resorting to Operation *Downfall*. The 509th CG had the components and assemblies for Fat Man, the second atomic bomb, at Tinian. The Manhattan Project personnel believed that this plutonium-239 device would make uranium-filled bombs, such as Little Boy, obsolete. Fat Man's explosive charge comprised some 13.5 lb of plutonium surrounded by gunpowder. Once the gunpowder was ignited, an implosive force magnified by a series of special lenses would compress the plutonium, bringing about the nuclear reaction. The design of this bomb was more complex than that of Little Boy, and technical problems, such as the development of the lenses, had necessitated a test detonation at Trinity. Fat Man was half the length of Little Boy, but weighed in at 10,900 lb. One area of concern was that its rotund shape caused aerodynamic instability, making the bomb wobble as it descended. As a result, the crew might not achieve an accurate drop.

THE PLAN OF ATTACK

Under Special Mission No. 16, the 509th would drop Fat Man on 9 August, on either the primary target of Kokura, or the secondary target of Nagasaki; both were located on Kyushu's west coast. Kokura's arsenal was a major source of automatic weapons and the city contained other arms and steel manufacturing centers. Kokura also featured shipbuilding and repair facilities. Nagasaki possessed four Mitsubishi plants that produced over 96 percent of all weapons production by plants with more than 50 workers. The city had suffered just five small bombing raids and appeared all but unscathed; it was a perfect example for a demonstration of Fat Man's power. Nagasaki also had shipyards that built and repaired maritime vessels.

Tibbets selected Major Charles Sweeney to pilot the B-29 *Bockscar* (references commonly refer to it as "*Bock's Car*") and deliver the device. Sweeney's aircraft bore the name of its regular pilot Captain Frederick C. Bock, Jr. Tibbets reassigned Bock to fly *The Great Artiste*, which still carried the scientific equipment from the Hiroshima attack. Bock carried a special British scientific team and William Laurence, the newspaper reporter who had been assigned to the Manhattan Project since its inception, to record the

The flight path of *Bockscar* to Kokura and Nagasaki

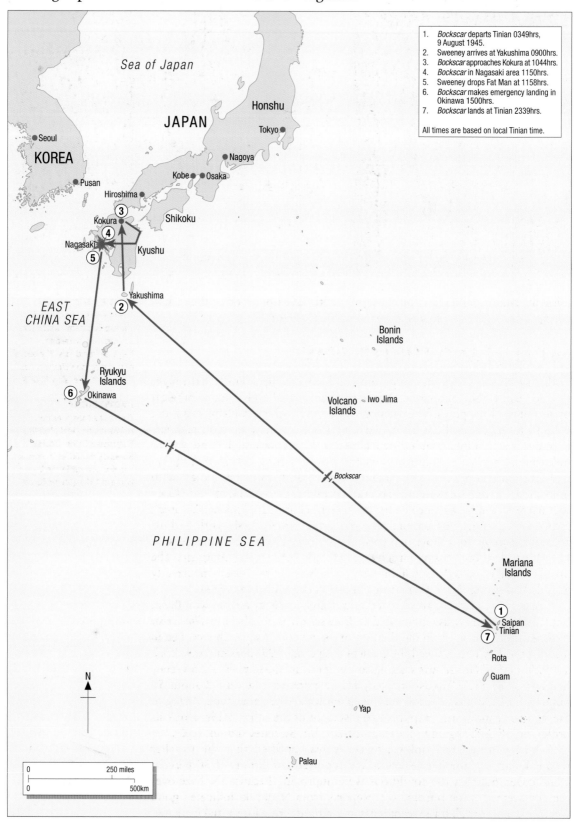

1. *Bockscar* departs Tinian 0349hrs, 9 August 1945.
2. Sweeney arrives at Yakushima 0900hrs.
3. *Bockscar* approaches Kokura at 1044hrs.
4. *Bockscar* in Nagasaki area 1150hrs.
5. Sweeney drops Fat Man at 1158hrs.
6. *Bockscar* makes emergency landing in Okinawa 1500hrs.
7. *Bockscar* lands at Tinian 2339hrs.

All times are based on local Tinian time.

Sea of Japan

Honshu

JAPAN

Tokyo

Seoul

KOREA

Nagoya

Pusan

Kobe   Osaka

Hiroshima

Kokura ③

④

Shikoku

Nagasaki ⑤

Kyushu

Yakushima

②

EAST
CHINA SEA

Bonin
Islands

Ryukyu
Islands

⑥ Okinawa

Volcano
Islands   Iwo Jima

Bockscar

PHILIPPINE SEA

Mariana
Islands

①
Saipan
Tinian

⑦

Rota

Guam

N

Yap

Palau

0   250 miles

0   500km

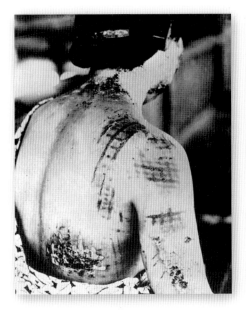

2ND ATOMIC BOMBER CREW
AUG 11, 1945

mission. Major James I. Hopkins, Jr., 509th CG operations officer, had control of the photographic support aircraft, *Full House*.

FAT MAN AND THE FORECAST

Ordnance crews loaded the plutonium bomb aboard the aircraft on the night of 8 August. USN Commander Ashworth armed the bomb prior to take-off by installing three plugs. The mission started off with a problem, and more were to follow. A typhoon near Iwo Jima forced USAAF mission planners to move the planned rendezvous between *Bockscar* and her escorts to Yakushima, an island south of Kyushu. Sweeney took off at 0349hrs on 9 August and headed north. Strong headwinds slowed her progress to Yakushima. Unfortunately, a photographic specialist assigned to *Full House* was barred from flying since he forgot his parachute. Hopkins had to break radio silence to get instructions to operate the camera. Ashworth and his assistant discovered a more dangerous situation; an indicator showed that Fat Man's electronic fusing circuits had closed with arming complete. The problem was a failed switch in which the wiring had been incorrectly installed, meaning that a premature explosion could have occurred.

The next problem happened over Yakushima. Sweeney met up with Bock, but failed to rendezvous with Hopkins. *Bockscar* would only have *The Great Artiste* to accompany it on the final leg of its mission. Ashworth recorded in his log that they had reached the rendezvous point at 0900hrs and saw Bock at 0920hrs. *Full House* was waiting south of the arranged position. Sweeney had agreed to circle Yakushima only for 15 minutes, but waited about 50 minutes for Hopkins to show up: this glitch wasted precious fuel. Owing to the weather conditions, Hopkins had lost sight of the other B-29s. Hopkins broke radio silence again to locate *Bockscar*, but Sweeney did not reply.

While waiting for Hopkins, Sweeney was notified that the weather reconnaissance plane over Kokura had reported conditions of 30 percent cloud cover, but that the conditions were improving because the haze over the city seemed to be burning off. Reports from Nagasaki indicated good weather conditions, but the reconnaissance aircraft crew forecasted increased

ABOVE, LEFT
The nuclear blast created widespread death and injury among Hiroshima and Nagasaki residents. The pattern of this woman's kimono was burned into her skin. (DOD)

ABOVE, RIGHT
Bockscar's crew returned to Wendover Field after the Nagasaki mission. Charles Sweeney would later retire as a major general in the US Air Force in 1976. (US Air Force)

The USAAF's dominance over Japan allowed unprecedented photographic intelligence over Nagasaki. (US Air Force)

1 TATEGAMI SHIPYARD
2 MITSUBISHI DOCKYARD
3 AKUNOURA ENGINE WORKS
4 MITSUBISHI ELECTRIC MFG CO.
5 NAGASAKI & DEJIMA WHARVES &
   R. R. YARDS
6 MITSUBISHI STEEL & ARMS WORKS
7 MITSUBISHI-URAKAMI ORDNANCE PLANT

cloudiness. Sweeney made the target choice: Kokura. He signaled to Bock to proceed to Kokura. The weather aircraft's presence had alerted Japanese air defenses to an enemy presence at 0845hrs and a raid alarm sounded at 0850hrs. The all-clear notification was sounded at 0930hrs though.

Bockscar reached the initial start point of her bomb run over the target at 1044hrs. Sweeney, like Tibbets, was under strict orders to use visual bomb delivery only. If they could not use this, their standing order was to return home with Fat Man. Fortunately for Kokura's residents, *Bockscar*'s bombardier, Captain Raymond "Kermit" Beahan, could not locate the aiming point since a heavy cloud cover had settled over the city. The crew attempted two more bomb runs. Antiaircraft artillery fire started up and enemy interceptors were located on the radar. One aviation mechanic/gunner claimed to see fighters flying towards the B-29.

After *Bockscar* had made three unsuccessful bomb runs, her flight engineer discovered a major malfunction: a fuel pump had stopped working, trapping 600 gallons of fuel in the auxiliary bomb bay fuel tanks. This fuel was now unavailable for use. If future problems occurred in flight, the aircraft might not be able to safely return home. The mission might have to be aborted and the plane diverted to Okinawa. Since Iwo Jima's airfield was closed, the crew could not transfer Fat Man to another B-29. *Bockscar* had spent 45 minutes of flight time over Kokura trying to drop Fat Man, using up more precious fuel. After consulting Ashworth and Beahan, Sweeney decided to continue on south to Nagasaki despite potential fuel concerns. If weather conditions did not improve, Sweeney was prepared to drop Fat Man using radar guidance, contrary to orders.

Bockscar and *The Great Artiste* flew on to Sagonoseki, a peninsula in northeastern Kyushu, to approach Nagasaki from the east. Sweeney managed to pilot *Bockscar* over Nagasaki at 1150hrs. Japanese air defense officials announced *Bockscar* and *The Great Artiste*'s high-altitude arrival with an air raid alert at 1153hrs. Disappointingly, the weather over Nagasaki was just as bad as at Kokura, with 70–80 percent cloud cover. The B-29's navigator used radar to reach the Nagasaki area. *Bockscar* reached the initial point to begin the bomb run to the aiming point. With cloud cover obscuring the area, the bombardier prepared for a radar bomb drop. Due to his shortage of fuel, Sweeney would make a single bomb run. At the last moment before using a radar approach, a hole in the clouds opened and exposed the aim point: the Mitsubishi Steel and Arms Works located on the Urakami River, north of the main city and about 1.6 miles from Nagasaki's harbor. The bombardier purportedly dropped Fat Man from *Bockscar* at 1158hrs (there is some dispute over the actual bomb release time). Sweeney was flying at 28,000ft and at an indicated air speed of 200 knots. Fat Man wobbled down and exploded about 1,650ft above the impact point after a descent of 50 seconds. Initial reports indicated that the explosion took place about 500 yards north of the Mitsubishi plant and about 0.8 miles south of another Mitsubishi facility.

Sweeney had made a hard 60-degree right bank and turned the aircraft about 155 degrees. The power of the detonation surprised the aircrew: Fat Man's estimated 22,000 pounds of TNT yield exceeded that of Little Boy. *Bockscar* and *The Great Artiste* suffered five successive shock waves. Sweeney commented that his B-29 shook as if it "were being beaten by a telegraph pole."

Down below in Nagasaki, the detonation created massive casualties and damage, but not as great as the lower-yield Little Boy. The city's geography played a major role in limiting Fat Man's effects, indeed it is estimated that up to 80 percent of Fat Man's power was dissipated. With the city surrounded by hills, the explosion was confined to the bowl-shaped center, in contrast to relatively flat Hiroshima and its suburbs. Nagasaki's estimated 1945 population was 195,000 people. Japanese officials compiled initial reports of 23,753 killed with 1,927 missing and 23,345 wounded. These reports underestimated the true losses. A June 1946 calculation estimated that Fat Man caused 39,000 deaths and 25,000 injured. The official USSBS pushed the fatalities to 45,000 and the injured from 50,000 to 60,000 a year later.

TOP
Fat Man was assembled on Tinian's North Field. *Bockscar* would carry it to Kokura, but then deliver it on Nagasaki. (National Archives)

BOTTOM
Bockscar delivered Fat Man over Nagasaki on 9 August 1945. The mission convinced Tokyo that the Hiroshima mission was not an isolated incident. (DOD)

NAGASAKI: AN UNLUCKY TURN OF EVENTS (pp. 72–73)

On 9 August 1945, the aircraft *Bockscar* **(1)** 509th CG dropped a second atomic bomb on Japan. The original target was Kokura, but poor visibility over the target forced a change to Nagasaki. The city was the third largest on the island of Kyushu and was a secondary target for the 9 August mission. Weather conditions were also poor over Nagasaki, but an opening in the clouds allowed the B-29's bombardier to see the aim point and drop Fat Man **(2)**, a plutonium-armed bomb.

Nagasaki had largely escaped the massive USAAF high-explosive and incendiary bombing raids that had devastated the country in previous months. Although the city had suffered five bombing raids, it did not sustain any major damage during these. The city's shipyards, steel works, industrial plants, electrical equipment factories, arsenals and other industrial sites offered a lucrative target to the USAAF.

Nagasaki's geography channeled much of the bomb's effects and, whilst still devastating, fewer casualties resulted than in Hiroshima. Fat Man's plutonium core exploded in the air above a point some 500ft south of the Mitsubishi Steel and Armaments Works.

F-13 photographic reconnaissance aircraft provided valuable intelligence information about the damage caused. Full steel production would be delayed for up to a year; weapons manufacturing would require 15 months of repair to restore production to two-thirds of full capacity; and the city's population had to wait at least six months for a return to normal electricity supply and service.

The attack convinced the Japanese emperor and many cabinet members to accept surrender. However, most Japanese military leaders were unconvinced and wanted to continue the war, but the emperor demanded their acceptance of the terms of the Potsdam Declaration. The raid had succeeded in demonstrating that the United States had the ability to continue using atomic weapons.

TOP, LEFT
After Nagasaki, the Japanese government accepted the Potsdam Declaration. The city was destroyed, and was completely rebuilt in the postwar period. (DOD)

BOTTOM, LEFT
The bomb blast damaged un-reinforced buildings, and fire swept through the city. The destruction caused by Fat Man is clearly evident. (DOD)

Along the Urakami River, Nagasaki's population density was higher than in Hiroshima or Tokyo. One study placed Nagasaki's casualty rate, based on thousands per square mile destroyed, much higher than at Hiroshima: 43,000 compared to 32,000. Mortality rates for Nagasaki, using the same methodology, peaked at 20,000 deaths per square mile while Hiroshima suffered 15,000 deaths. To aid comparison, Tokyo's March 9/10 1945

A – Diameter of mushroom cloud at 30 seconds after detonation (15,000ft high)
B – Diameter of mushroom cloud at 60 seconds after detonation (35,000ft high)

35,000FT

28,000FT
(PLANE ALTITUDE)

15,000FT

▼ EVENTS

1 Having failed to bomb Kokura, *Bockscar* and *The Great Artiste* begin their approach run to the secondary target of Nagasaki from 100 miles to the city's east.

2 *Bockscar* drops Fat Man at 1158hrs from an altitude of 28,000ft. The aim point is the Mitsubishi Steel and Arm Works.

3 Sweeney in *Bockscar* banks 60 degrees and executes a 155-degree right turn.

4 Bock in *The Great Artiste* executes a 155-degree left turn.

5 After a 50-second descent, Fat Man explodes 1,650ft above Ground Zero, some three-quarters of a mile from the aim point. The city's geography channels and dissipates much of the blast.

6 *Bockscar* and *The Great Artiste* are struck by five successive shock waves after the explosion.

7 *Bockscar* and *The Great Artiste* make one orbit of the city at a range of 11 miles from the hypocenter, and then head for Okinawa at 1205hrs with a mere 300 gallons of fuel left.

8 The mushroom cloud moves east; as it does so, a sticky, black rain begins to fall onto the area below.

NAGASAKI, 9 AUGUST 1945

The routes of *Bockscar* and *The Great Artiste* during the mission to drop Fat Man over Nagasaki. Having failed to bomb the primary target of Kokura due to heavy cloud cover, Sweeney headed for Nagasaki. The 22-kiloton plutonium device detonated some 50 seconds after it was dropped.

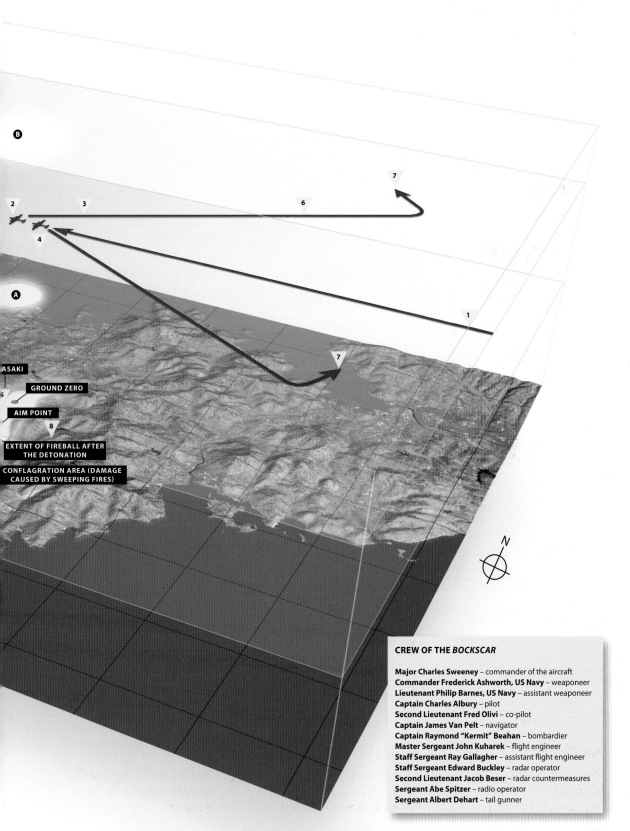

Note: gridlines are shown at intervals of 2 miles/3.2km

B

A

NAGASAKI

GROUND ZERO

AIM POINT

EXTENT OF FIREBALL AFTER
THE DETONATION

CONFLAGRATION AREA (DAMAGE
CAUSED BY SWEEPING FIRES)

CREW OF THE *BOCKSCAR*

Major Charles Sweeney – commander of the aircraft
Commander Frederick Ashworth, US Navy – weaponeer
Lieutenant Philip Barnes, US Navy – assistant weaponeer
Captain Charles Albury – pilot
Second Lieutenant Fred Olivi – co-pilot
Captain James Van Pelt – navigator
Captain Raymond "Kermit" Beahan – bombardier
Master Sergeant John Kuharek – flight engineer
Staff Sergeant Ray Gallagher – assistant flight engineer
Staff Sergeant Edward Buckley – radar operator
Second Lieutenant Jacob Beser – radar countermeasures
Sergeant Abe Spitzer – radio operator
Sergeant Albert Dehart – tail gunner

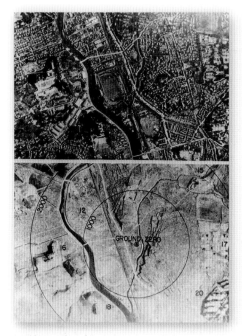

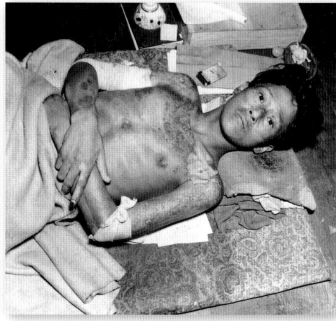

incendiary raid killed 5,300 per square mile and the average of 93 urban attacks resulted in only 1,000 deaths under the same conditions.

Bomb damage to physical structures was erratic at Nagasaki. Some areas suffered great destruction, while adjacent locations seemed almost untouched. The main area of destruction took an oval form, running north–south along the Urakami River, about 2.3 miles wide and about 1.9 miles long. Fat Man destroyed about 1.45 square miles of the city out of an estimated 3.84 square miles, much less than at Hiroshima. Sweeney's mission wiped out an estimated 68.3 percent of pre-existing industrial production, excluding the harbor facilities. Despite the damage, the single north–south National Railway track was not seriously disrupted. Traffic into and out of the city was able to proceed. Fortunately for Nagasaki's residents, and in contrast to events at Hiroshima, winds and the local conditions did not create a firestorm. One might imagine what would have happened if Fat Man had exploded over Hiroshima instead. Still, postwar USSBS analysis indicated that the raid on Nagasaki was the equivalent of a raid of about 120 B-29s. Although Fat Man's debut was notable, by itself it was no more destructive than other comparable B-29 incendiary night raids.

Having circled Fat Man's growing mushroom cloud once, Sweeney headed towards Okinawa at 1205hrs. His task now was to nurse his B-29 to a landing site with only 300 gallons of fuel. *Bockscar*'s radio operator notified air-sea rescue of the possibility of a ditching at sea. Fortunately for *Bockscar*'s crew, they returned to Yontan Field in Okinawa with seven gallons of fuel left, and headed back to Tinian later that day.

AFTERMATH

Soviet army officers had begun their campaign planning for an invasion of Japanese-held Manchuria as early as March 1945. They would use a double envelopment to crush the Japanese Kwangtung Army and take Manchuria, before driving into Korea. By April, Soviet military strength had doubled along Manchuria's borders. Soviet armored forces comprised over 4,700 tanks and about 1,850 self-propelled guns. Opposing the Soviets, the Japanese Kwantung Army had 713,000 men and 1,155 obsolete tanks, and there were only 50 aircraft available. On 9 August 1945, Soviet army forces invaded Manchuria, across three fronts: the Trans-Baikal (654,040 personnel), First Far East (586,589 men) and Second Far-East (a 337,096 strike force) fronts.

The Japanese government was facing overwhelming problems that day. Sweeney had delivered Fat Man on Nagasaki; Hiroshima had been proven not to be an isolated experiment. How many bombs the United States had was debatable, but Truman's willingness to use these weapons provided a new, larger threat to homeland defense. Moscow had spurned all possibilities of helping Tokyo negotiate a peace with the Allies by declaring war. The IJA now had another front on which to fight, facing Soviet veterans transported from Europe after their victory over Germany. Soviet air forces attacked targets across Northeast Asia, including Manchurian and North Korean cities and Japanese convoys in the Sea of Japan. IJA units across the area facing a Soviet invasion were weak and could not possibly stem any major offensive, which might lead to the fall of Northeast Asia, Sakhalin, the Kuril Islands and then Hokkaido. Tokyo had stripped men and equipment for homeland defense and the likelihood of stopping the Soviets was low. Spaatz had used diversionary B-29 raids to draw attention from Nagasaki on 9 August by sending 165 bombers to strike Amagasaki, a port between Kobe and Osaka and the Tokyo area. Tactical and medium-range bombers could now hit Japan. Carrier task forces and surface ships could sail Japan's east coast to bombard her cities just as War Plan Orange envisioned. As Japanese strength ebbed, Allied force structure increased. Despite war weariness, America was building up her military strength for continued bombing and an invasion, most probably on Kyushu.

The crisis propelled Prime Minister Suzuki and the Japanese cabinet into heated debate. On 9 August, Suzuki attempted to get the War Minister General Anami Korechika and the Chief of the Army General Staff General Umezu Yoshijiro, hardline militarists, to accept the Potsdam Declaration. Anami was adamant that he would not surrender. Japanese military personnel for years had held surrender to be unacceptable and Anami would not change

On 10 August 1945, Emperor Hirohito met with the Japanese cabinet. While Hirohito (center) listens to the arguments, Prime Minister Suzuki (standing) addresses the cabinet. Foreign Minister Togo sits across from Suzuki (at the head of the table). (US Army)

his mind now. Suzuki and the militants could only agree that if there were any surrender, then it should ensure that the "national polity" or imperial family would continue in any postwar settlement. Anami and Umezu pushed for further, more favourable conditions. First, Japan would demobilize and disarm any IJA or IJN forces overseas. Second, Japanese courts would prosecute any war criminals. Third, after surrender the Allies would not occupy Japan. Chief of the Navy General Staff, Admiral Toyoda Soemu, agreed with Anami and Umezu. Togo and Navy Minister Admiral Yonai Mitsumasa disagreed. Togo believed that a declaration of pre-conditions would sabotage any hope of quickly ending the war. Washington might put harsher conditions on the surrender terms in retaliation. Home Minister Abe Genki told the cabinet that the Japanese rice crop would be the poorest in 15 years. The Allied blockade of Japan had taken its toll on food imports. Industry had ground to a halt due to blockade and bombing. Food riots and social collapse might occur if Tokyo accepted unconditional surrender. The cabinet was deadlocked.

The cabinet could only act in a unanimous manner to make policy decisions. Although Hirohito could theoretically make law, he did not use his powers on a daily basis, but used the cabinet to work out details and report to him. Military officers, like Anami, had the ability to veto decisions. Despite heavy losses in Okinawa, continued conventional bombing, the atomic bombs and the Soviet attacks into Manchuria, the IJA resisted surrender. The IJN leadership, without any meaningful surface and carrier fleet, was less unified in opposing a peaceful solution. The only means to break the impasse was to directly involve the emperor in the process. Around 0200hrs on August 10, the cabinet met with the emperor. Hirohito agreed with Togo to accept the Potsdam Declaration. He saw no need to continue the war since the military had not completed the necessary defensive fortifications nor armed newly formed units for homeland defense. Failed promises by the IJA and IJN in the past had reinforced Hirohito's thoughts that the military

could not deliver victory. He ordered that the nation stop any further military efforts and start the surrender process. All in attendance agreed unanimously. By 0700hrs, the Japanese government, through Swedish and Swiss intermediaries, sent an offer to accept the Potsdam Declaration, with one proviso: Japan would retain Hirohito as its sovereign ruler.

The Japanese now awaited Washington's response. Tokyo had released a public statement to her citizens that "we must admit our fortunes are at their lowest ebb." The statement did not directly admit to accepting the Potsdam Declaration or any moves towards surrender, but was readying the population for the inevitable. IJA and IJN high-level commanders started to hear about the surrender. Commanders like Vice Admiral Ugaki Matome, Commander-in-Chief of the Fifth Air Fleet, refused to accept the idea that Japan would surrender, reflecting the popular military choice to fight on.

Washington's initial response to the Japanese offer came on 12 August at 0100hrs. A radio transmission stated that the emperor and the Japanese government, once surrender had taken place, would be "subject to the Supreme Commander of the Allied Powers"– Douglas MacArthur. This provision seemed to skirt the issue of any future imperial system. However, the response again included the statement that Japan's future form of government should be "established by the freely expressed will of the Japanese people." Another concern was the health and safety of the 168,500 Allied prisoners of war held by the Japanese. A top priority for Marshall and Truman was their swift and safe release.

US Secretary of State James F. Byrnes, a critic of the Japanese imperial system, carefully crafted the response to Tokyo's 10 August offer. Unconditional surrender was still the accepted policy. A unilateral alteration of the Potsdam Declaration would appear as being soft on the Japanese, which might cause an international and domestic outcry. The Soviet and Chinese governments wanted abolishment of the Japanese imperial system. Truman could not back down. Churchill had tried to moderate the unconditional surrender condition, but failed. Conversely, America's rejection of a peace offer might also bring protests. Stimson wanted to accept the peace offer immediately since he believed that, without an organized surrender supported by the emperor, his forces would have to fight "a score of bloody Iwo Jimas and Okinawas" all over China and Southeast Asia.

The Japanese military, despite huge losses, still had a large force, albeit with equipment deficiencies. After the surrender, MacArthur's staff projected that the Japanese military forces totaled 6,983,000 soldiers, sailors and airmen throughout the empire. IJA and IJN forces stationed in the home islands accounted for 3,532,000 members of the military. Without IJA and IJN immediate capitulation, rogue military commanders might continue resistance. If the invasions occurred, then surrender might be bloodier than expected. Additionally, if the United States wanted a speedy reconstruction under orderly conditions, the imperial system could help administer and ease a transition of the nation's social, military, political and economic conditions. Everyday government and social functions might cease while the Allies reconstituted basic services. Chaos would ensue and a successful Japanese reconstruction might take years and tremendous resources. Keeping Hirohito would assist Allied efforts to keep a compliant populace. Giving the Japanese the opportunity to select their form of government was guaranteed in the Potsdam Declaration; if the Japanese wanted to retain their emperor they could and probably would. Byrnes merely reiterated the declaration's provisions.

Secretary Byrnes, in the future, would also have to deal with the Soviets in postwar Asia. An overly harsh rejection of the Japanese surrender offer might delay any settlement. If the Soviets crushed Japanese forces in northeast Asia and started an invasion of northern Japan, then administration and reconstruction of Japan between MacArthur as Supreme Commander of Allied Powers and his Soviet counterpart might be difficult. The United States might face a divided country, like it did in Germany. A weakened postwar Japan might affect the spread of communism in the Far East by forcing the United States to concentrate on her rebuilding whilst not watching other areas in Asia or the Pacific.

Japanese reaction to the surrender was mixed. Togo viewed the clause about the choosing of a postwar government as a choice to keep the imperial

Civilians throughout the United States celebrated wildly on hearing of Japan's capitulation. Only those military personnel earmarked to take part in Operation *Downfall* were probably more pleased at the news. (DOD)

system. Anami, Umezu, Toyoda and Abe thought it did not answer the question. Suzuki started to waver. Heated debate ensued once again. A key adviser to the emperor, Marquis Kido Koichi, Lord Keeper of the Privy Seal, supported Togo's efforts and was very influential in getting Suzuki to support acceptance of Byrnes' reply. Japanese peace advocates feared any questioning of the American response would bring an immediate and negative severance of future negotiations and relations. Anami also met with Kido over his objections concerning Byrnes' direct response to the imperial system's future. Fortunately, Anami did not resign from the cabinet. If he did, Tokyo would need to form a new cabinet, which would delay and possibly sink any attempt to surrender.

Several IJA officers committed to resisting any surrender to the Americans developed a plan. Suzuki and others had feared a mutiny among military members unless the IJA and IJN senior leadership would quash any defiance to Hirohito's acceptance of the Potsdam Declaration. Anami and some officers from the War Ministry and Army General Staff met on 13 August at 2000hrs to hear a *coup d'état* plot that would take over the government and continue the war. The conspirators wanted Anami's approval, but the War Minister delayed any decision.

The next day, USAAF and US Navy aircraft launched the biggest strategic aerial raid on Japan to date. Truman was concerned about Japan's stalling over Byrnes' reply. Over 1,000 USAAF bombers struck the country, with 833 B-29s taking part in the attack. Some aircraft also dropped leaflets that detailed the Potsdam Declaration, Japan's offer to surrender and Washington's reply. Tokyo's attempt to keep its citizens unaware of the negotiations was exposed. It was clear that Tokyo was facing more incendiary and conventional bombing attacks and possibly more atomic ones. Japanese military leaders had the will to fight, but Japan's capability was weakening daily. Imperial Japanese military forces could fight on, but for what purpose? The nation would be destroyed. The added concerns about Soviet intervention, the spotlight placed on Asia and the Pacific with Germany's fall, an impending invasion, relentless conventional air and naval attacks, fears of mass starvation and the potential rain of atomic bombs on Japanese cities was too much for the emperor. There was no other option, but to surrender and hope for merciful treatment by the Allies.

Kido presented one of the leaflets to Hirohito and urged him to accept unconditional surrender. Kido feared that the militarists might seize control over the armed forces and fight on to Japan's destruction. Emperor Hirohito summoned the cabinet and the highest-ranking field commanders in Japan: Hata, Sugiyama and Fleet Admiral Nagano Osami. Hirohito wanted the senior field commanders to accept and to ensure obedience to any decision to surrender. Despite Anami's, Umezu's and Toyoda's resistance, the emperor prevailed and told the cabinet conditions had not changed since 10 August. He would accept Washington's conditions and tell the public via a radio broadcast about this. Hirohito would record his message for later replay. By 2300hrs, Togo transmitted an imperial rescript of surrender, via the Swiss and Swedish governments, to the Allied governments. Japan had admitted defeat.

The Japanese senior military leadership immediately sent directives to all personnel to follow the imperial rescript. Obedience was expected from all subordinates. Despite these moves, some *coup d'état* conspirators decided to seize the emperor's phonographic recording. During the evening of 14/15 August, several field grade officers sought to take control of the Imperial Palace and isolate Hirohito. Others would take over the central radio station to stop any broadcast. For the conspirators, time might allow resistance to surrender among military members to grow. To take the palace, they assassinated the commander of the Imperial Guards Division who protected the emperor. The plot failed to retrieve the recording and support for the *coup d'état* was stillborn, since senior officers refused to take part. The emperor was never harmed during the incident. Anami, from whom the conspirators tried to gain support, had already decided to commit suicide. By 0800hrs on 15 August, the plot to seize the government was over, and the ringleaders killed themselves. Other senior military leaders would do the same over the decision to surrender. Suzuki and Kido were targets of assassination, but they survived. Ordinary Japanese citizens heard Hirohito explain the surrender at noon on 15 August. Suzuki and the other cabinet members resigned. The war was over. General Prince Higashikuni Naruhiko became prime minister. While certain IJA and IJN commanders begged him to continue the war, Higashikuni wisely declined.

Washington received news of the surrender via a Japanese news broadcast. Truman was relieved that the Japanese had accepted the unconditional surrender terms. The Allies and the Japanese now began the process of ending the hostilities. The two sides coordinated an exchange of prisoners of war, demobilization, disarmament, occupation of the home islands and other activities before a formal surrender could be signed. On 2 September, at 0855hrs, a Japanese delegation boarded the USS *Missouri* in Tokyo Bay. MacArthur presided over the formalities. The Instrument of Surrender was signed within 20 minutes and formalities ended at 0920hrs. Umezu, who opposed surrender, represented the IJA and IJN and signed the document. Japanese forces surrendered throughout the Pacific, relinquishing their last major stronghold of Singapore on 12 September.

THE FUTURE OF WARFARE

Europe had become quickly divided soon after Germany's surrender. Allied governments had set up occupation zones, which separated Germany into American, British, French and Soviet sectors. Similarly, Eastern Europe had fallen under the Soviet sphere of influence and control. Truman had managed to avoid this problem in Japan by getting Tokyo to surrender before the Soviet Union could lay claim and occupy any major Japanese home island territories. Truman's choice to use the atomic bomb was one of the key strategic decisions in World War II, which not only affected military activities, but had a profound impact on postwar policies and relations between nations. While Roosevelt

The end of the war was accompanied by a display of American airpower over the USS *Missouri* in Tokyo Bay on 2 September 1945. (US Navy)

and Truman had not generally interfered with specific military decisions made during World War II, the last campaign to end the war was different and its wider objectives and significance were far greater than previous ones. If the Japanese government did not succumb and accept Allied terms, then the United States and her Allies might have to fight Japanese forces throughout mainland Asia and in isolated Pacific outposts, actions that might take years and raise the cost in terms of casualties and resources to new heights. The stakes were too great to leave to just another purely military operation.

Warfare had been fought with traditional land and naval forces for millennia. As weapons technology improved, the advent of the aircraft and with it new munitions and delivery systems had changed the nature of warfare. Although nations had experimented with strategic bombardment in World War I, the prospect of winning a war through airpower alone had gained limited credence at the outbreak of World War II. Payloads were small, precision was lacking and any damage caused was comparatively limited unless massed attacks were used. However, by the summer of 1945, the new weapon that emerged from the laboratory added a new and terrifying dimension to airborne warfare. Landing and losing thousands of ground forces to destroy a key target was no longer necessary. The United States could now threaten the destruction of a capital city or other target without a long, bloody campaign now that the will and ability to drop the atomic bomb had been demonstrated. Nuclear weapons had the capability of vaporizing whole cities, and no existing defense mechanism could stop this.

Although the events of August 1945 ended World War II, many postwar issues were created at the same time. Some writers have argued that the United States used the atomic bombs to influence Moscow to affect postwar relations. Countries that could develop a nuclear weapon and delivery system could gain immediate recognition as a regional or world power that could destroy a rival. A nation's international status and prestige could increase immeasurably through this action without having to build a large conventional military. Washington's use of nuclear weapons launched the atomic age. The desire of nation states to build a nuclear weapon for national pride, to serve as a deterrent, or as a substitute for a costly conventional force defined the second half of the 20th century and the opening decade of the 21st; several countries have or are in the process of developing small-yield nuclear weapons in the range of Little Boy or Fat Man. Although they pose little threat globally, they are still very troublesome to their regional neighbors, and, in the age of terrorism, the control of such weapons is a vexing concern.

The Potsdam Conference helped unify the United States, Britain, China and the Soviet Union to forge an alliance to defeat Japan. These actions gave the United States assurance that the Soviets would tie down hundreds of thousands of Japanese forces in mainland Asia. Unfortunately, giving the Soviets the ability to place major military forces in northeast Asia also had significant implications for postwar concerns. Soviet expansion and influence helped communist forces in China and allowed a totalitarian North Korean government to form. One might speculate what the world would have looked like if communist forces had not taken over China or North Korea. Truman would later have to answer charges about losing China and would have to wage three years of bitter conflict in Korea. These actions also gave Stalin the ability to develop a greater Soviet presence in Asia and the Pacific for the future.

Paul Tibbets and the 509th CG also provided a vision to leading defense strategists about future warfare. World War II was costly in terms of manpower and budget resources. By 1945, the United States supported over 12,056,000 men and women on active duty. Washington also paid for 2,628,000 federal civilian workers to assist the uniformed force. By 1944, national defense spending was over 37.8 percent of the United States' gross domestic product. America had not returned to a prosperous economic state owing to the 1929 global depression and World War II. The public wanted a rebuilt, stronger economy, and politicians heard this cry. Despite America's sudden thrust to the front of global affairs to ensure a peaceful world, the call to reduce government expenditures and look inward was hard to dismiss. Maintaining peace with fewer ships, tanks and planes would be difficult, but not impossible. Perhaps a great reliance on nuclear weapons might reduce pressure on the defense budget.

America's two operational atomic missions had demonstrated much greater levels of destruction than ever seen before. Instead of years to conquer an enemy, it might take hours or in some cases minutes. Nuclear missions were sought by all services. Delivery systems, more powerful nuclear weapons, command and control systems and other related activities began to get higher priorities than conventional weapons. Doctrine and strategies started to change, emphasizing nuclear deterrence and move and countermove. Strategy was part art and part science, always with the fear

When IJA and IJN units surrendered in September 1945, some tried to redeem their honor by destroying regimental flags rather than turning them over to the Allies. (US Army)

that a major conflict could spill over to a nuclear one. The days of creating a single War Plan Orange were in stark contrast to the hundreds of options and variations of postwar strategic planning. Civilian and military strategists planned for all contingencies and faced a new war: the Cold War. America could no longer afford a slow mobilization of her military, economy and people to fight Moscow or one of her client states in a global conflict that could destroy the nation or its allies. Military units had to be ready to fight at a moment's notice, especially with nuclear weapons.

If the United States had hoped to return to simpler times, then the public and the government were mistaken. The United States had global responsibilities in 1945. Europe needed Washington's resources and her help to rebuild after years of war. Asia and the Pacific also saw few options that did not include the United States as a partner in national security issues. In Japan, MacArthur would later rebuild the government, economy and even society. He pressed for and got a new constitution, laws, labor unions and other reforms to reshape the land.

Demobilization of the millions of active duty members in the United States began shortly after Japan's surrender. Unlike other wars in the past, the nation now had a large-scale presence overseas, because of defense commitments or reconstruction. Some congressional leaders wanted a return to prewar international relations, with the country free from foreign entanglement. Active military strength was only 458,000 in 1940, but American military commitments would support an additional two to three million personnel during the 1950s and 1960s. Washington's military presence in Europe and now the Far East secured its future role, whether she sought it or not, in these two volatile regions. Protecting Japan became paramount after the establishment of the People's Republic of China and the Korean War. Japan has continued to this day as a strategic outpost for American national interests in the Pacific.

Despite heavy damage to Japan's cities following the nuclear and conventional bombing raids, Japan was able to be rebuilt. An opposed invasion and subsequent Japanese fight to the death would have devastated the country and created lengthy delays to returning the country to any sense of

A sticking point of the surrender terms was the demobilization of Japan's military. Japanese soldiers are shown here returning home by train from Hiroshima in September 1945. (DOD)

normality. With the acceptance of unconditional surrender, MacArthur became the civil administrator and highest-ranking military commander in Japan. Instead of landing with invading troops, MacArthur was faced with a different and in many ways more difficult task. He would have to democratize Japanese politics; restructure the economy, abolish the war industry and find a way to redistribute land; administer the country and redefine the emperor's role; give humanitarian aid; and provide security. In short, MacArthur had to create a new, peaceful Japan, and would succeed in doing so. Fortunately for General of the Army Douglas MacArthur, once Hirohito told his people to follow the wishes of MacArthur few problems with security ensued and reform took place. Some 354,675 American troops would be stationed throughout the country by December 1945.

The events of August 1945 did not entail the complete destruction of Japan. If an invasion had occurred with continued blockade and bombing, then Japan might have suffered even greater damage. Hirohito's acceptance of unconditional surrender led to an end to war and, in some ways, a faster reconstruction of Japan. This effort was very successful and allowed Japan to prosper. MacArthur achieved the end objective of creating a non-belligerent Japan that offered no threat to her neighbors. Her peaceful nature has continued to the present day, which is due to the many social, economic, legal and political changes following World War II. By 1945 Allied military, diplomatic and other personnel had the foresight to consider many of these postwar issues and their impact on Japan. Japan became an example where democracy and nation-building efforts clearly succeeded. One of the Allies' objectives to free people from a future of tyranny had finally been realized.

THE SITES TODAY

Anyone interested in tracing the atomic bomb's development and use or the later stages of the Pacific War can visit several interesting locations. In the United States, several sites with links to the atomic bomb are open to the public. The 509th CG's training site at Wendover Field is located about a half mile south of Wendover, Utah on the state border between Nevada and Utah. The site is accessible from I-80 and is about 106 miles west of Salt Lake City. The Wendover Airfield Museum has maintained some of the facilities, restored field equipment and operates several displays. One can take a base tour of its runways and the facilities. The museum is open daily from 0800hrs to 1800hrs. For current information visit the website at www.cr.nps.gov /nr/travel/aviation/wen.htm.

Another interesting location is the National Museum of Nuclear Science and History (formerly the National Atomic Museum), which includes historical and technical exhibits, including one on the Manhattan Project, and specific displays on the Little Boy and Fat Man weapons. The museum is in Albuquerque, New Mexico north of the Old Town section at 1905 Mountain Road, NW. The museum is open daily from 0900hrs to 1700hrs (except New Year's Day, Easter, Thanksgiving and Christmas Day); there is an admission fee. One can find more information about this unique museum at www.atomicmuseum.com.

Los Alamos National Laboratory, site of the design and test work for the Manhattan Project, operates the Bradbury Science Museum. Los Alamos continues to conduct research on a number of national security projects,

Bockscar today is fully restored at the National Museum of the US Air Force in Wright-Patterson AFB, Ohio. (US Air Force)

including nuclear weapons. This site features weapons exhibits, including Little Boy and Fat Man and explanations of key technologies. Admission is free and the site is open from 1000hrs to 1700hrs on Tuesday to Saturday and 1300hrs to 1700hrs on Sunday and Monday. The museum is closed on New Year's Day, Thanksgiving and Christmas Day. Los Alamos is within driving distance north from Albuquerque using Interstate 25. Further details can be found at www.lanl.gov/museum.

More adventurous visitors may want to visit the desolate Trinity Fat Man test site at the US Army's White Sands Missile Range. This remote site is open twice a year, on the first Saturdays in April and October. One can see ground zero (the location over which the test plutonium bomb exploded), an instrumentation bunker, base camp and other facilities. White Sands Missile Range maintains a web site, www.wsmr.army.mil/pao/TrinitySite/trinst.htm. The site has few amenities and visitors are warned about the lack of such support.

One might also want to see the *Enola Gay*. The National Air and Space Museum's Steve F. Udvar-Hazy Center, near Dulles International Airport in the greater Washington, DC area, houses this famous B-29 and other Pacific War-period aircraft. The museum is accessible from the intersection of Virginia State Routes 28 (Sully Road) and 50. Admission to the museum is free, but there is a parking fee. The museum is open daily from 1030hrs to 1730hrs, except Christmas Day. Additional information can be found at www.nasn.si.edu for this facility and the museum on the National Mall in downtown Washington, DC.

The crew of *Enola Gay*, with Colonel Paul Tibbets at center, after their return to Tinian from Hiroshima. The aircraft has since been restored and is located at the Steve F. Udvar-Hazy Center of the National Air Museum near Washington, DC. (US Air Force)

The City Commercial Display remains today as a visible reminder of the dropping of Little Boy on Hiroshima. The building is commonly called the "A-Bomb Dome" and is located near ground zero. (Clayton K.S. Chun)

Individuals wanting to see a superior collection of military aircraft can go to the National Museum of the United States Air Force at Wright-Patterson AFB, Ohio, near Dayton. The museum contains *Bockscar* and many examples of World War II Pacific Theater aircraft. Admission is free and the facility is open from 0900hrs to 1700hrs, except on New Year's Day, Thanksgiving and Christmas Day. One can easily reach this site from Interstates 70, 75, or 675. The museum has an annex located within the base that requires a form of government-issued photo identification to visit.

The USS *Missouri*, located in Hawaii at Pearl Harbor Naval Station, provides a great opportunity to see a World War II battleship and the site of the 2 September 1945 signing of the Instrument of Surrender of Japan to the Allies. The ship is located near the USS *Arizona* Memorial and offers the visitor the ability to see two key vessels of the Pacific War. The USS *Missouri* offers several tours on a paid admission basis. The United States National Park Service operates the USS *Arizona* Memorial, which tells the story of the 7 December 1941 raid at Pearl Harbor. Both tourist attractions can be very crowded during peak tourist seasons in the summer, Christmas and spring. The USS *Bowfin,* a World War II-era submarine, is also located near the *Arizona* Memorial and allows visitors to see one of the boats that helped blockade Japan. The *Bowfin* Museum and the submarine charge a fee for admission.

Another little-known site is Tinian's North Field, which is a National Historic Landmark. If you can get to Tinian, you can see some of the landing beaches that American forces used to take the island. Interested visitors can see the loading pits used to place Little Boy and Fat Man on board the B-29s for delivery over Hiroshima and Nagasaki. The most convenient way to visit the island is by flying from Guam to Tinian, about 45 minutes, and most sites are easily accessed from the airport. There are no organized tours of North Field.

The cities of Hiroshima and Nagasaki have been largely rebuilt and have sprung back to life, even around the ground zero areas. Hiroshima offers a number of visitor locations. In downtown Hiroshima, a prominent site to visit is the Hiroshima Peace Memorial Museum, near the location below Little Boy's detonation. The museum features several displays that illustrate and interpret the Hiroshima atomic bomb raid from a Japanese viewpoint. Transportation is readily available by bus or streetcar. The facility has seasonal hours to visit the exhibits, and a small admission fee is charged. Near the museum are various monuments dedicated to the casualties from the raid and a structure that survived the attack. The Commercial Display Building (or "A-bomb Dome") is a visible reminder of the impact of Little Boy.

The other major Japanese museum is the Nagasaki Atomic Bomb Museum. The building includes exhibits about the damage caused by Fat Man to Nagasaki and the postwar nuclear age. The museum is near a major train station (JR Nagasaki Station) and the nearby Peace Park. Paid admission allows the visitor to see a graphic display of a Japanese interpretation of the events leading up to the Nagasaki raid and its aftermath.

BIBLIOGRAPHY

Allen, Thomas B. and Norman Polmar *Code-Name Downfall: The Secret Plan to Invade Japan – and Why Truman Dropped the Bomb* (New York, Simon and Shuster, 1995)

Buckley, John *Air Power in the Age of Total War* (Bloomington, IN: Indiana University Press, 1999)

Cline, Ray S. *Washington Command Post: The Operations Division* (Washington, DC: Center of Military History, 1990)

Crane, Conrad C. *Bombs, Cities, & Civilians: American Airpower Strategy in World War II* (Lawrence, KS: The University Press of Kansas, 1993)

Craven, Frank Wesley and James Lea Cates *The Army Air Forces in World War II: Volume Five, The Pacific: Matterhorn to Nagasaki June 1944 to August 1945* (Chicago, IL: University of Chicago Press, 1953)

Drea, Edward J. *MacArthur's ULTRA: Codebreaking and the War Against Japan, 1942–1945* (Lawrence, KS: University Press of Kansas, 1992)

Frank, Richard B. *Downfall: The End of the Imperial Japanese Empire* (New York, Random House, 1999)

Goldstein, Donald M., Katherine V. Dillon and J. Michael Wenger *Rain of Ruin: A Photographic History of Hiroshima and Nagasaki* (Washington, DC: Brassey's, 1995)

Group Historian *History of 509th Composite Group, 313th Bombardment Wing, Twentieth Air Force: Activation to 15 August 1945* (Tinian, 31 August 1945) (declassified)

Hall, Cargill R., ed. *Case Studies in Strategic Bombardment* (Washington, DC: Air Force History and Museums Program, 1998)

Headquarters IX Corps *Field Order 1 Operation Olympic* (12 August 1845) (declassified)

Headquarters USAFFE and Eighth US Army (Rear) *Homeland Air Defense Operations Record* (Japanese Monograph 157) (Washington, DC: Office of the Chief of Military History, 1958)

_____ *Homeland Operations* (Japanese Monograph 17) (Washington, DC: Office of the Chief of Military History, 1958)

Huston, John W., ed. *American Airpower Comes of Age: General Henry H. "Hap" Arnold's World War II Diaries Volume 2* (Maxwell AFB, AL: Air University Press, 2002)

Jones, Vincent C. *Manhattan: The Army and the Atomic Bomb* (Washington, DC: Center of Military History, 1985)

Kreis, John F. (ed.) *Piercing the Fog: intelligence and Army Air Forces Operations in World War II* (Washington, DC: Air Force History and Museums Program, 1996)

MacEachin, Douglas J. *The Final Months of the War with Japan: Signals Intelligence, US Planning and the A-Bomb Decision* (Washington, DC: Center for the Study of Intelligence, 1998)

Maddox, Robert James *Weapons for Victory: The Hiroshima Decision Fifty Years Later* (Columbia, MO: University of Missouri Press, 1995)

Maga, Tim *America Attacks Japan: The Invasion That Never Was* (Lexington, KY: The University Press of Kentucky, 2002)

Marston, Daniel (ed.) *The Pacific War Companion: From Pearl Harbor to Hiroshima* (Oxford: Osprey Publishing, 2005)

Matloff, Maurice *Strategic Planning for Coalition Warfare 1943–1944* (Washington, DC: Center of Military History, 1959)

Miller, Edward S. *War Plan Orange: The US Strategy to Defeat Japan, 1897–1945* (Annapolis, MD: Naval Institute Press, 1991)

O'Connor, Raymond (ed.) *The Japanese Navy in World War II* (Annapolis, MD: Naval Institute Press, 1971)

Potter, E.B. *Nimitz* (Annapolis, MD: Naval Institute Press, 1976)

Rees, David *The Defeat of Japan* (Westport, CT: Praeger, 1997)

Rhodes, Richard *The Making of the Atomic Bomb* (New York: Simon and Schuster, 1986)

Skates, John Ray *The Invasion of Japan: Alternative to the Bomb* (Columbia, SC: University of South Carolina Press, 1994)

Spector, Ronald H. *Eagle Against the Sun* (New York: Free Press, 1985)

Supreme Commander, Allied Powers (Japan), General Staff *Reports of General MacArthur: Japanese Operations in the Southwest Pacific Area Volume II* (Part I and II) [n.d.]

Thomas, Gordon and Max Morgan Witts *Enola Gay* (Old Saybrook, CT: Konecky & Konecky, 1977)

US Army Operation *Olympic* Microforms D767.2.064 1994 (Ft. Leavenworth, KS: Combat Arms Research Library, 1944-1947)

US Army Forces in the Pacific *Staff Study Operations: Olympic* (General Headquarters, US Army Forces in the Pacific, 1945) (declassified)

_____ *G-2 Estimate of the Enemy Situation with Respect to an Operation Against Southern Kyushu in November 1945* (Military Intelligence Section, 25 April 1945) (declassified)

_____ *"Downfall": Strategic Plan for Operations in the Japanese Archipelago* (General Headquarters, US Army Forces in the Pacific, 28 May 1945) (declassified)

US Strategic Bombing Survey, *The U.S Strategic Bombing Survey, 1945-1947* Various Volumes (Washington, DC, n.d.)

INDEX

References to illustrations are shown in **bold**.